THIF

ESSENTIAL LIFE SKILLS SERIES

WHAT YOU NEED TO KNOW ABOUT

READING SIGNS, DIRECTORIES, SCHEDULES, MAPS, CHARTS & GRAPHS

Carolyn Morton Starkey

Norgina Wright Penn

National Textbook Company

NTC a division of *NTC Publishing Group* • Lincolnwood, Illinois USA

ACKNOWLEDGMENTS

Ameritech, area code map'
General Drafting Co., Inc., Baltimore and Detroit maps. Copyright ©
General Drafting Co., Inc. All rights reserved.
Michigan Bell Telephone Co., excerpts from Yellow Pages
Harold Washington Library Center, Chicago Public Library, floorplan
Wisconsin Department of Transportation, state maps

1995 Printing

Preface

This third edition from the Essential Life Skills Series tells you what you need to know about reading directories, signs, maps, schedules, and graphs. Mastering these skills will make you more assertive and self-confident. You will learn to cope better with everyday situations.

This book covers some familiar yet very important materials. You will learn to read, write, and understand:

floor plans	maps
building directories	schedules
telephone books	charts
street and highway signs	graphs

Throughout the book you will find examples of real directories, signs, maps, schedules, and graphs, like the ones you see and use everyday.

Each section in this book includes definitions of words that may be new or difficult. Checkup sections help you review what you have learned. There are many opportunities to practice your skills. "Show What You Know" activities offer you the opportunity to apply your new skills.

Because of its flexible format, this book can be used either for self-study or in a group setting with an instructor. The answer key is on perforated pages so that it is easy to remove.

When you have mastered the skills in this book, you will want to develop other skills to become more successful in our modern world. The other books in the Essential Life Skills Series will show you how.

Essential Life Skills Series

What You Need to Know about Reading Labels, Directions & Newspapers
0-8442-5169-0

What You Need to Know about Reading Ads, Reference Materials & Legal Documents 0-8442-5170-4

What You Need to Know about Getting a Job and Filling Out Forms
0-8442-5171-2

What You Need to Know about Reading Signs, Directories, Schedules, Maps, Charts & Graphs 0-8442-5172-0

What You Need to Know about Basic Writing Skills, Letters & Consumer Complaints 0-8442-5173-9

Contents

Using Directories and Floor Plans

Special Reading Strategies

Using Directories and Floor Plans

When you look up numbers in a telephone book, you use a directory. When you read a list of departments in a store, you use a directory. A shopping mall or library may display floor plans with directories. These help you find locations or information fast. Directories can save you time.

In this section, you will practice using directories and floor plans.

Directories and floor plans

WORDS TO KNOW

annex an addition to a building

directory a listing of names and addresses

floor plan a drawing showing the size and arrangement of rooms on each floor of a building

mezzanine a low story between two main stories in a building, usually above the ground floor, sometimes in the form of a balcony

Directories are alphabetical listings. Sometimes they are in book form, like the telephone book. Sometimes they are in display form, like those in department stores. They help you find an address or a phone number. They help you find which floor an office is on. They help you locate what you want in a big store. Directories are arranged in several different ways.

Some directories are simply alphabetical lists. The white pages of the telephone book is one such alphabetical list. In the white pages you can find telephone numbers listed by a person's last name. You can also find business listings under the name of the business.

Another way to arrange a directory is to list the floors of a store or office building in order, then to list items by their floor location. Another way is to use section headings, such as the sections of a shopping mall.

A floor plan is both a map and a directory. With a floor plan you get both a list of items *and* a drawing. Floor plans can be very helpful for buildings with a number of stores, offices, or departments.

ACTIVITY 1
Using store directories

Department store directories are usually arranged like the directory below. Use this directory of Morton's Bargain City to locate the items listed below. On which floor would you find each of these items?

Morton's Bargain City

	Floor		Floor
Appliances	1	Infants' Wear	3
Books	2	Lingerie	2
Cafeteria	2	Luggage	1
Children's Wear	3	Men's Wear	2
Cosmetics	2	Office Supplies	1
Kitchen and Bath	3	Shoes	2
Handbags	2	Toys	1
Infants' Furniture	3	Women's Wear	2

1. Baby Crib _____

2. Baby Doll _____

3. Makeup _____

4. Woman's Dress _____

5. Man's Shirt _____

6. Boots _____

7. Dishwasher _____

8. Index Cards _____

9. Purse _____

10. Baby Blanket _____

11. Lunch _____

12. Cookware _____

13. Novel _____

14. Hosiery _____

15. Bicycle _____

16. Clothes Dryer _____

17. Typewriter _____

18. Woman's Blouse _____

19. Place mats _____

20. Stroller _____

21. Refrigerator _____

22. Bath Towels _____

23. Nightgown _____

24. File Folders _____

25. Coffee Maker _____

26. Sneakers _____

27. Briefcase _____

28. Hair Dryer _____

29. Man's Tie _____

30. Baseball Bat _____

ACTIVITY 2
Using a floor directory for a department store

This is a floor directory. A floor directory is often found on or near the elevators of large department stores. It lists each floor. It also lists what may be found on each floor. Use the sample floor directory to answer the questions below.

MAIN FLOOR
Girl's Wear
Women's Wear

SECOND FLOOR
Accessories
Boy's Wear
Budget Dresses
Ladies' Lounge

THIRD FLOOR
Alterations
Coats
Men's Wear
Men's Lounge

FOURTH FLOOR
Furniture
Carpeting

FIFTH FLOOR
Housewares
Silverware

SIXTH FLOOR
Beauty Salon
Pillows, Linen, Bedding

SEVENTH FLOOR
Personnel Office/Credit
Restaurants
    On Top
    Ice Cream Parlor

On which floor would you get off the elevator if . . .

1. you wanted to pay on your charge account? _____

2. you wanted to price a microwave oven? _____

3. you were on the fifth floor and you wanted to go to the nearest rest room? _____

4. you were Jennifer Mallory and you wanted to pick up your husband's suit? _____

5. you were Tom Mallory and you promised to meet Jennifer on the carpet floor? _____

6. you were looking for a small appliance to give as a wedding gift? _____

7. you had an appointment at the store's "Sophisticated Scissors" beauty salon? _____

8. you were looking for furniture for your new apartment? _____

9. you wanted to apply for a job as a salesperson? _____

10. you wanted a chocolate sundae? _____

ACTIVITY 3
Using building directories

This is the building directory for The Enterprise Tower. It lists all offices in the building. Use this directory to answer the questions below:

Building Directory

	Floor		Floor
Acme Enterprises	10	Kilpatrick Construction	8
Armstrong Gallery	10	Kroop Advertising	2
Barclay Consultants	10	LeGrand, J. S., M.D.	6
Bartlett & Bartlett Law Offices	10	Lerner, Gwen, M.D.	6
Bear & Bear Job Consultants	8	Longman Employment	3
Boston, Harry E., D.D.S.	7	Martin, W. E., M.D.	6
Brown, Boveri, & Barton Corp.	10	Martin Wholesalers	8
C&H Associates	2	Marvel Photos	4
Carteret Bank	3	Mondi Exports	8
Christens, Nancy, M.D.	6	Morrison, Patricia, D.D.S.	7
Claytor, Harold, M.D.	6	Neal & Neal Consultants	2
Cutler, Stanley, Attorney	5	Neptune Unlimited	3
Cyrus, Lynette, Attorney	5	Nile Products	10
D'Angelo, Kenneth, M.D.	6	O'Shea, Matthew, M.D.	6
Daniels Realty	2	Rosenberg Studios	2
Daniels, Sandra, M.D.	6	Sanchez, Dorothy, D.D.S.	7
Designer Fur Headquarters	3	Sanchez, Louis, D.D.S.	7
Family Health Center	6	Santiago, Louis, M.D.	6
Ferrell Employment Agency	4	Sibeski Brothers	5
Flynn & Flynn Accounting	4	Tami Studios	5
Goldman, Ronald, M.D.	6	Technical Labs	2
Green, Terry Phillip, M.D.	6	Tutor Computers	2
Green, Thomas, M.D.	7	Tutor Electronics	2
Higgins, Higgins, & Higgins	8	Tyler Textiles	8
Ingram Consultants	9	Wong's Distributors	10
International Banking Inc.	10	World Enterprises	10
International Publishing	10	World Health Inc.	6
J&E Imports	10	World Publishers	8
J&W Exports	10	Young Galleries	2
Jones & Jones Enterprises	9	Zee, Pauline, M.D.	6

1. On which floor will you find J&E Imports? _____

   J&W Exports? _____

2. On which floor will you find the legal offices of Bartlett & Bartlett? _____

4

3. Does Dr. Harold Green have an office in this building? _____

4. Does Dr. Ronald Goldman have an office in this building? _____

5. On which floor is Wong's Distributors? _____

6. Is Kroop Advertising located in this building? _____

7. What listing comes *before* Dr. W. E. Martin's name? _____

8. What listing comes *after* Dr. Martin's name? _____

9. If this directory is on the first floor, how many floors will you have to walk up in order to visit the Young Galleries? _____

10. If you were on the 5th floor and used the elevator to go to Dr. Terry Green's office, how many floors up would you travel? _____

11. On what floor is Dr. Lerner? _____

12. The first number of the office numbers in the Tower tells you what floor the office is on. Complete the *room numbers* of these offices:

    a. Dr. Harry Boston   _____ 08

    b. Sibeski Brothers   _____ 02

    c. Dr. Harold Claytor   _____ 11

    d. Dr. Sandra Daniels   _____ 13

    e. Dr. Patricia Morrison   _____ 07

    f. Dr. Pauline Zee   _____ 05

    g. World Enterprises   _____ 13

    h. Tami Studios   _____ 10

Floor plans Using a floor plan is like using a map. Floor plans help you find your way. They help you in malls, shopping plazas, and office buildings. The key to reading a floor plan is knowing whereyou are.

You must find your location on the floor plan. Then you can locate other places. Decide if your destination is in front or in back of you. Decide if it is to your left or right. See if it has a name or number. See if there is a pattern to the floor plan. Is it an L-shape? Is it a circle? Is it in sections? Are there section numbers?

ACTIVITY 4
Using floor plans

Study the floor plan of the third floor of the Harold Washington Library Center, the Chicago Public Library and answer the questions below.

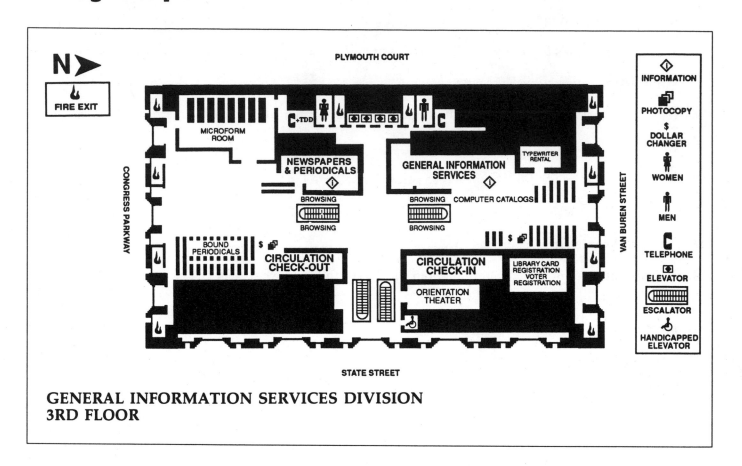

GENERAL INFORMATION SERVICES DIVISION
3RD FLOOR

1. If you walk from Circulation Check-in to General Information Services, in which direction will you be walking? _____

2. How many photocopiers are on this floor? _____

3. Can you get to the Orientation Theater if you are in a wheelchair? _____

4. Can you look up the title of a book on this floor? _____

5. If you get off an elevator on the west side, which two directions will you walk to the Voter Registration Desk? _____

6. How many fire exits are there? _____

7. Is the fiction section on this floor? _____

8. Could you find a newspaper on this floor? _____

The directory below lists the stores in the Town & Country Mall. The floor plan shows the locations of the businesses. Use the directory and the floor plan to answer the questions.

Business Directory

Allen Patton's Pets A–5	Eaton's A–8
Avenue Fashions B–4	Harrison's Men's Shop B–3
Burgers Deluxe B–1	Jim's Jewelry A–2
Carolyn's Boutique A–7	Kid's World A–6
Charles's Chop House A–10	Martin's Travel A–9
Chinese Cuisine A–4	Norge's Portraits B–2
Daisy's Donut Shop A–1	Vicky's Hat Rack A–3

A–5	A–6	A–7	A–8

A–4
A–3
A–2
A–1

Main Floor

A–9
A–10

You Are Here

B–1
B–2

Mezzanine

B–4
B–3

1. Are the businesses in the directory listed by types of business or alphabetically? _____

2. Will you walk right or left to find Chinese Cuisine? _____

3. Is Eaton's right or left of Carolyn's Boutique? _____

4. Is Harrison's Men's Shop on the main floor or on the mezzanine? _____

5. Where will you stop if you want a donut? _____

6. Where could you get your picture taken? _____

The telephone book

Knowing how to find information in the phone book is a useful everyday skill. There are many times when you need to use the phone book. You may need to find a name, an address, or a telephone number. The telephone book has two sections. They are the white pages and the yellow pages. In larger cities, the white pages and yellow pages are separate books.

The white pages

Most people are familiar with the white pages of the phone book. This is where you find the telephone numbers of people you want to call. Businesses might also list their numbers in this section, but the white pages are mainly for home listings.

The white pages are easy to use if you understand how they are arranged.

Fernandez - Filbert

Fernandez, Lola 141 State St	555-8332
Fernandez, M. 4245 Burt Rd.	555-7899
Fernandez, M.L. 223 Orange Bl	555-8254
Fernandez, Martino	
8610 Gladstone Av Bloomfield	555-4149
Filbert, Abbott 61 N Park Pl	555-7083
Filbert, Alvin 2109 2nd Av	555-3321
Filbert, Bertha 18 Lane Dr	555-2578
FILBERT TOOL & DIE CO	
44 Main Lane	555-8866
Filbert, Stanley 621 Cherry St	555-5461

1. The white page listings are arranged in alphabetical order with last names first.
2. Businesses might appear in the same alphabetical listings.
3. Each white page listing consists of a name, address, and telephone number.
4. Addresses will often be abbreviated. (For example, "N" for north, "Rd" for Road, "Pk" for Park.)
5. Headings are at the top of the white pages. They tell you the first and last names on a page.

ACTIVITY 5
Reading the white pages

Use the white page listings on the previous page to answer these questions.

1. What is the number for Lola Fernandez?

2. What is the number for Martino Fernandez?

3. What is the number for Filbert Tool & Die Co.?

4. What number do you call to reach Alvin Filbert on 2nd Ave.?

5. What number do you call to reach M. Fernandez at 4245 Burt Rd.?

6. What is the number for M. L. Fernandez on Orange Blvd.?

ACTIVITY 6
Locating telephone numbers for persons with the same names

Sometimes white-page listings are confusing. Names may be similar or even the same. Answer the questions about the telephone listings below.

Jones · Jones

Jones Della 1676 Grassylawn Drive	555-8421
Jones Dwight 8989 Rhine Rd	555-2813
Jones E 171 Lois Lane	555-8210
Jones E 6 S. Ohio Ave	555-9828
Jones E 712 Colorado Blvd Farmington	555-7241
Jones E 7918 St. Agnes	555-6471
Jones E A 817 Marked Dr	555-0010
Jones E C 230 Van Born Rd	555-3331

Jones E S 2001 Main St	555-6666
Jones Earl, MD 923 Derby Lane	555-3245
Jones Earl 44 Pine St Ferry Pk	555-7110
Jones Earl 18095 Steel St	555-7808
Jones Earlie 1409 Raleigh St	555-4648
Jones F 106 Wyoming Blvd	555-5523
Jones F 614 Greenlawn Ave	555-6010
Jones Fred 601 Wright Pl	555-7041

1. What number do you call to reach Dwight Jones?

2. If you are trying to reach Dr. Earl Jones, what number do you call?

3. What number do you dial if you are trying to reach E. Jones at 7918 St. Agnes?

4. How many Earl Joneses are shown?

5. What is the number for the Earl Jones in Ferry Park?

6. What number do you dial to reach E. C. Jones on Van Born Rd?

The yellow pages   The yellow pages of your phone book list the names, addresses, and phone numbers of businesses. Doctors, lawyers, and dentists are also found in the yellow pages. But there are no residential listings. Businesses appear in both the white pages and the yellow pages, but the yellow pages give more information about the services these businesses provide.

The yellow pages are a handy reference. Look at the yellow page sample on page 12. To use the yellow pages, you need to understand how they are arranged.

1. Businesses are listed under the service, product, or specialty they offer. Examples are RESTAURANTS, PLUMBING, AIR-CONDITIONING, AUTO SALES, and PHYSICIANS.

2. These headings, showing the service, product, or specialty, are arranged alphabetically.

3. Under these headings, the names of the businesses appear in alphabetical order.

4. Each listing consists of the name, address, and telephone number, just as it does in the white pages, but these listings are under a heading. For example, Smith's Garage is not under "S" for Smith. It is under GARAGES or AUTOMOBILE SERVICE.

5. Many of these yellow page listings also appear as advertisements. These ads give more information about a business. They may give hours, location, and directions.

ACTIVITY 7
Deciding when to use the yellow pages

Answer these questions about the yellow pages.

1. If you are a shopper, what are some benefits of looking for a business in the yellow pages? (Name at least three.)

   _____

   _____

   _____

2. John Watts owns a VCR. He needs to have it repaired. Should he look in the white pages or yellow pages for a repair shop?

   _____

3. You want Carlos' Car Repair to give your car a tune-up. You know where the repair shop is. But you need the telephone number to call for an appointment. Would you use the yellow pages or the white pages?

   _____

   Explain your answer.

   _____

   _____

   _____

ACTIVITY 8
Classifying yellow-page listings

Below are yellow page headings that deal with furniture and automobiles. These headings are lettered. Stores are also listed. Decide under which heading each store belongs.

a. FURNITURE DEALERS - RETAIL
b. FURNITURE RENTING & LEASING
c. FURNITURE REPAIRING & REFINISHING

_____ 1. Universal Refinishers

_____ 2. The Restore

_____ 3. Quality Furniture

_____ 4. Flex-A-Lease, Inc.

_____ 5. I.F.G. Furniture Rentals

_____ 6. Frank's Used Furniture Store

_____ 7. Scandinavian Furniture

_____ 8. American Furniture Rentals

_____ 9. Mitchell Upholstery

_____ 10. Imported Oriental Furniture

Now classify the car businesses listed below under the correct yellow page heading.

a. AUTOMOBILE BODY REPAIRING & PAINTING
b. AUTOMOBILE DEALERS - ANTIQUE & CLASSIC
c. AUTOMOBILE DEALERS - NEW CARS
d. AUTOMOBILE PARTS & SUPPLIES
e. AUTOMOBILE RADIOS & STEREO SYSTEMS

_____ 1. Smith's Car Parts

_____ 2. Clark Auto Parts, Inc.

_____ 3. Pierre's Classic Cars, Inc.

_____ 4. Vintage Vehicles, Inc.

_____ 5. Bob's Hubcap Specialists

_____ 6. J & G Automotive Parts

_____ 7. Dan's Body & Fender Shop

_____ 8. Dependable Auto Parts Store

_____ 9. A & E Auto Supply

_____ 10. George's Body Shop

_____ 11. Central Chevrolet

_____ 12. Autosound, Inc.

_____ 13. Glenbrook Ford, Inc.

_____ 14. Bill's Auto Painting

_____ 15. Sound Experience, Inc.

_____ 16. Chrysler-Plymouth Sales

ACTIVITY 9

Reading and understanding the yellow pages

Use these yellow-page listings to answer the following questions.

Cleaners—Cont'd

Advertisers at this heading are required by law to be licensed.
(See Page A)

DeLUXE DRY CLEANERS PLANT
Main Plant Bay At Weiss
2700 Bay Sag **792-8779**
FENT'S LAUNDRY CENTER
9141 E Birch Run BrchRn..**624-9698**
Frankenmuth Cleaners Inc
160 S Main Frkmth.......652-2551
GEORGE'S DRY CLEANERS

"Serving Saginaw Since 1945"

**QUALITY WORK
ONE DAY SERVICE**

In By 10 A.M. Out By 4 P.M.
Just East Of N. Michigan On Shattuck

509 Shattuck Rd Saginaw...**754-8543**

Giant Wash-O-Matic & Dry Clng
2320 Webber Sag....... 755-5064
GOODWILL CLEANERS
SUDDEN SERVICE
IN BY 10 AM OUT BY 4 PM
402 N Mich Sag...........**754-6112**
1900 Hess Sag Plant.......**753-4401**
GUIDA DRY CLEANERS

| PICK-UP AND DELIVERY | **GUIDA** QUALITY CLEANING |

Serving Saginaw For Over 60 Years
1 Day Service On Request
★ Alterations
★ Button Replacements
★ Zippers Repaired
★ Leather Cleaning
★ Drapery Cleaning
COMPLETE SHIRT SERVICE

DIAL 754-9793

700 Lapeer Saginaw

JACOB'S CLEANING VILLAGE
2714 Center Av Essex.....**893-6191**
MR SUDS DRY CLEANING

**SUEDE & LEATHER
SERVICES**

• Cleaning   • Zippers
• Re-Dyeing   • Mending
• Re-Styling   • Leather
• New Linings   Buttons

CALL 755-5700

2319 Webber   Saginaw

Mr Suds Laundry & Professional Dry Cleaners
1215 E Genesee Sag..... 754-2063
3860 Dixie Sag...........777-9954
O & O Fabric Care Center
1000 Columbus ByCy.....894-2281

PHYL'S ONE HOUR MARTINIZING

DRY CLEANERS

Draperies • Leathers
Shirt Service • Wedding Gown
Preservation • Repairs & Alterations

(Drive-Up Window)

3416 State Saginaw......**792-7861**

QUERBACH LEATHER PROCESS INC
Insist On Professional Care For All
Your Leathers · Weekly Pick-Ups At
Your Cleaners Where Signs Displayed
M-40 North Allegan ...**616 673-8140**

REALGOOD CLEANERS

*"A LITTLE BETTER —
A LITTLE MORE CAREFUL"*

ASK ABOUT OUR CASH & CARRY
DISCOUNT — ALTERATIONS
& REPAIRS - EXPERT SHIRT SERVICE
DRAPERY CLEANING SPECIALISTS
WITH PERFECT PLEAT METHOD
FOLDED & READY TO HANG

Retain Original Beauty To Your
Drapes - Loc-Tite Stretch "N" Pleat
Draperies Taken Down and Hanging
Service Available With Cleaning

MAIN OFFICE - 793-6511

1317 COURT — SAGINAW

SHIELDS OFFICE - 781-0270

7871 GRATIOT — SAGINAW

ROTH DRY CLEANERS
2526 Broadway ByCy.... 892-2573
(See Advertisement This Page)
SALZBURG CLEANERS INC
Dry Cleaning & Shirt Service
1906 S Erie ByCy.......**893-5567**
3417 Center Av Rd Essex... 892-9070
(See Advertisement This Page)
Spotless Cleaners
1516 S Mich Sag....... 799-5161
(See Advertisement This Page)
State Street Dry Cleaners
4742 State Sag........ 793-7444
Steven's Dry Cleaning
3393 S Huron Rd ByCy....686-0911
**SUBURBAN DRY CLEANERS &
SHIRT LAUNDERERS**
• 1 Hr Service On Request
• Shirt Laundry
• Drapery & Leather Cleaning
• Storage
• Alterations & Reweaving

6853 Gratiot Saginaw.....**781-3650**

**SUDDEN SERVICE CLEANERS
& SHIRT LAUNDERERS**
1-HOUR DRY CLEANING SERVICE
2 Drive-In Windows
412 Wash By Cy.........**893-0071**

---

1. What is the type of business found on this page? _____

2. What is the *first* alphabetical listing on this page? _____

3. What is the *last* alphabetical listing on this page? _____

4. Did any listings under the same heading come *before* this page?

   _____

5. Are the businesses on this page providing products or a service? _____

   Some of the listings give more than telephone numbers and addresses. These listings appear in boxes. They tell about the services and sometimes the hours of the business. They are called classified-ad listings. Refer to these ads in answering the remaining questions.

6. What place cleans wedding gowns?

   _____

7. Name three places that clean leather.

   _____

   _____

   _____

8. Which cleaner replaces buttons?

   _____

9. Which cleaner will take down your drapes?

   _____

ACTIVITY 10
Choosing the yellow pages or the white pages

Classify the items below according to where they are most likely found—yellow pages, white pages, or both.

a. WHITE PAGES
b. YELLOW PAGES
c. BOTH

_____ 1. Jones, Charles

_____ 2. Bambi Department Store

_____ 3. Acme Printing Company

_____ 4. Smith, T. J.

_____ 5. Chun King Restaurant

_____ 6. Posey, Ernest

_____ 7. Central Television Repair Shop

_____ 8. Restaurants—Italian

_____ 9. Penn, Carolyn

_____ 10. Banks

_____ 11. Robinson, Charles, M.D.

_____ 12. Poison Control Center

_____ 13. Lawson, E. J.

_____ 14. Lawson Brothers Realty

_____ 15. James, Fred

_____ 16. Interior Decorators

_____ 17. Smith's Transfer

_____ 18. Chi Mer Restaurant

_____ 19. Wilson, John T. (attorney)

_____ 20. A & B Clothing

The area code map

The United States is divided into telephone dialing areas. Each area has an area code. This is a three-digit number. You use this number to dial long distance. For example, you want to call 555-2364 in South Carolina. But you live in Utah. You must dial 1 first and then the area code. It is 803. So you must dial 1, 803, and then 555-2364. When you do not know an area code, you can use the area code map in your telephone book. The map divides the United States into time zones. Notice that when it is 1:00 in California, it is 4:00 in Michigan.

ACTIVITY 11
Reading area code maps

Study the following area code map. Use this map to answer the following questions.

1. Give the area codes for   Arizona _____   Wyoming _____

South Dakota _____   Utah _____

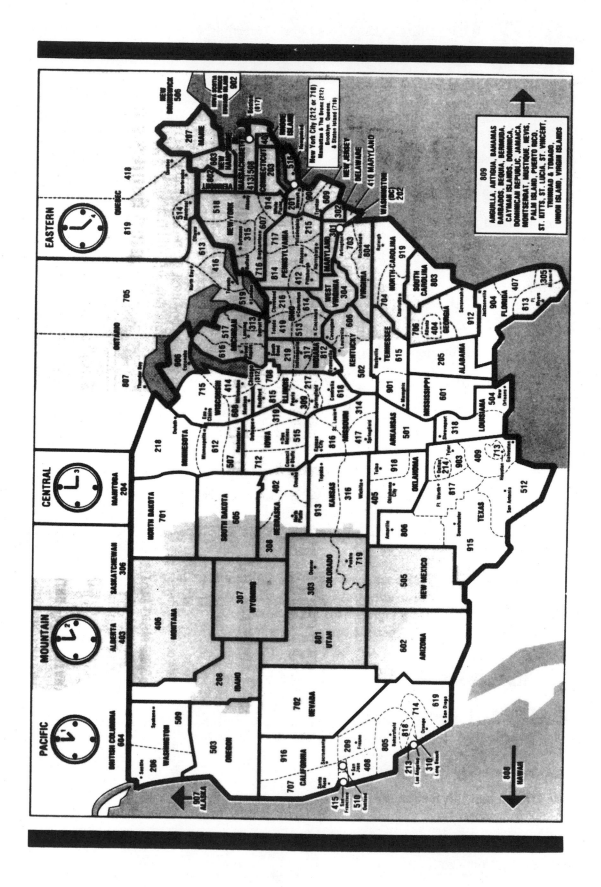

Courtesy of Illinois Bell–An Ameritech Company, 1992.

2. Give the area codes for Alaska ⎯⎯⎯⎯⎯⎯ Bermuda ⎯⎯⎯⎯⎯⎯⎯⎯⎯⎯⎯⎯⎯⎯⎯

   Hawaii ⎯⎯⎯⎯⎯⎯⎯⎯ Puerto Rico ⎯⎯⎯⎯⎯⎯⎯⎯⎯⎯⎯⎯⎯

3. Give the area codes for Ontario, Canada ⎯⎯⎯⎯⎯⎯⎯⎯⎯⎯⎯⎯⎯⎯⎯⎯⎯⎯⎯

   Quebec ⎯⎯⎯⎯⎯⎯⎯⎯⎯⎯⎯⎯⎯⎯⎯⎯⎯⎯⎯⎯⎯

   Saskatchewan ⎯⎯⎯⎯⎯⎯⎯⎯⎯⎯⎯⎯⎯⎯⎯⎯⎯

4. How many dialing areas (area codes) are in the state of Florida? ⎯⎯⎯⎯⎯⎯⎯⎯⎯

   West Virginia? ⎯⎯⎯⎯⎯⎯⎯⎯⎯

   Georgia? ⎯⎯⎯⎯⎯⎯⎯⎯⎯

   Montana? ⎯⎯⎯⎯⎯⎯⎯⎯⎯

   Texas? ⎯⎯⎯⎯⎯⎯⎯⎯⎯

5. What city in Texas is in the 512 area? ⎯⎯⎯⎯⎯⎯⎯⎯⎯⎯⎯⎯⎯⎯⎯⎯⎯⎯⎯⎯

   the 713 area? ⎯⎯⎯⎯⎯⎯⎯⎯⎯⎯⎯⎯⎯⎯⎯⎯⎯⎯⎯⎯

   the 214 area? ⎯⎯⎯⎯⎯⎯⎯⎯⎯⎯⎯⎯⎯⎯⎯⎯⎯⎯⎯⎯

6. If you wanted to make a long distance call to Philadelphia (Phila.), Pennsylvania, from out of state, what

   area code would you dial before the number? ⎯⎯⎯⎯⎯⎯⎯⎯⎯⎯⎯⎯⎯⎯⎯⎯⎯⎯

7. If you wanted to call Atlanta, Georgia, what area code would you dial? ⎯⎯⎯⎯⎯⎯⎯⎯⎯⎯

ACTIVITY 12
Reading area code maps

The area code map is divided into four time zones. They are Pacific, Mountain, Central, and Eastern. Screened areas indicated the four different geographical areas. Read each of the situations below. Decide which statement is correct. Also answer each time question.

Situation 1

You live in Seattle, Washington. At 9:01 A.M., you make a business call to New York City. You want to catch Jim Brown, the president of Lyons Construction, as soon as he arrives at work. The office hours are 9 to 5.

When you call, the secretary tells you:

⎯⎯⎯ **A.** Mr. Brown just left for lunch.

⎯⎯⎯ **B.** the office just opened and Mr. Brown should be in shortly.

⎯⎯⎯ **C.** the office is closing, call tomorrow.

What time is it in New York? ⎯⎯⎯⎯⎯⎯⎯⎯⎯⎯⎯⎯⎯⎯⎯⎯⎯⎯⎯⎯⎯⎯⎯⎯⎯⎯⎯

Situation 2

John Johnson calls his insurance company in Des Moines, Iowa. The person who answers the phone tells him that his agent, Mr. Brown, will be in at 3:00. John is calling from Maryland. When John calls back, his watch reads exactly 3:00.

But the receptionist tells him:

_____ **A.** his agent is at lunch from 12 to 1:00.

_____ **B.** call back at 4:00.

_____ **C.** call back in an hour.

What time is it in Des Moines? _____

CHECK YOUR UNDERSTANDING OF THE TELEPHONE DIRECTORY

1. A listing for The Skillful Carpenter is under what letter in the white pages? _____

2. Under what heading in the yellow pages would you most likely find The Skillful Carpenter?

   _____

3. You want to know which bus line has a route to Phoenix. What heading do you look up in the yellow

   pages? _____

4. How do you find a plumber in the yellow pages? _____

5. You want to call your friend Jason Pierce. You look under the letter _____ in the white pages.

6. You live in Chicago, Illinois. You want to call your friend in Los Angeles, California, at 8:30 in the

   morning, California time. What is the time in Chicago when you make the call? _____

7. You are at work in New York City. You place a business call to Houston, Texas. It is 1:00 P.M. in New
   York. In Houston:

   _____ **a.** the workday is over   _____ **b.** it is the lunch hour   _____ **c.** the workday has not begun

8. Put the following names in alphabetical order. Names beginning with *Mac* or *Mc* are alphabetized letter
   by letter. So all the *Macs* come before the *Mcs*.

   McNeil ____   MacDonald ____   Miner ____   Mack ____   Major ____   McKay ____

9. What does the abbreviation Av. mean? _____

10. Why might Dr. Gilbert Brown, Dentist, have two numbers listed after his name in the white pages?

   _____

2

Special reading strategies

Often information you need will require special reading skills. You may have to interpret a sign, symbol, or drawing. You may have to make comparisons using a chart or graph. You may have to read a schedule.

This chapter gives you practice in using everyday reference skills. First you will learn how to identify street and highway signs. Then you will read trail, street, and highway maps. You will practice reading bus, train, and plane schedules, and you will interpret line, bar, and circle graphs.

Street and highway signs

WORDS TO KNOW

guide signs   signs that show exits, distances, and directions, such as route numbers

maximum speed   the fastest speed allowed

minimum speed   the slowest speed allowed

obstruction   something that is blocking the road

pedestrian   a person who is walking

regulatory signs   signs that give information about traffic laws such as speed limits

right-of-way   the right to go first

service signs   signs that point out services such as rest stops, telephones, and gas stations

warning signs   signs that give warnings or cautions about possible dangers such as low bridges or sharp curves in a road

Street and highway signs carry important messages for drivers. They tell them the traffic laws. They warn of possible dangers ahead. They give distances and directions. They even direct drivers to telephones, gas stations, and rest stops.

Street and highway signs are grouped in three categories. They are REGULATORY SIGNS, WARNING SIGNS, and SERVICE AND GUIDE SIGNS.

Regulatory signs These signs show speed limits and other traffic regulations. Most regulatory signs are white with black letters.

Traffic in the right lane must turn right. Traffic in the left lane may go straight or turn right.

Drivers should keep to the right of an obstruction.

This sign is posted over a turning lane. Traffic from both directions uses this lane.

SPEED LIMIT 55 MINIMUM 45

The fastest safe speed is 55 miles per hour. The minimum safe speed is 45 miles per hour.

DO NOT PASS   PASS WITH CARE

These signs mark Passing and No Passing zones.

Sometimes a message on a regulatory sign is very important. This sign will be red with white letters.

This sign means come to a complete stop.

The driver *does not* have the right-of-way. Slow down and let right-of-way driver go first.

Don't drive onto any street or enter any highway with this sign.

You are driving the wrong way on a freeway, ramp, or street. You may meet another car.

A red circle with a line through it always means NO.

NO RIGHT TURN

NO TRUCKS

Some regulatory signs are for pedestrians also. NO HITCHHIKING is an example. Can you think of others?

ACTIVITY 1
Identifying regulatory signs

Match the signs with their meanings.

A.

B.

C.

D.

E.

F.

G.

H.

I.

J.

_____ 1. No "U" turn.

_____ 2. No trucks allowed.

_____ 3. This sign means the opposite of "Go."

_____ 4. Slow down. Be prepared to stop for drivers who have the right-of-way.

_____ 5. Turning lane.

_____ 6. Stay out!

_____ 7. Maximum safe speed.

_____ 8. You're driving in the wrong direction.

_____ 9. Keep to the right of an obstruction.

_____ 10. No right turn.

Warning signs   Warning signs are yellow with black letters. They're usually diamond-shaped.

Sharp curve ahead. Take curve at 35 mph.

Crossroads or side roads ahead. Watch for other vehicles entering, leaving, or crossing highways.

A bridge or underpass ahead. Clearance is 12 feet 6 inches.

Traffic light ahead. Be prepared to stop.

Traffic island or obstruction ahead. Drive to either side.

Reminder: two-way highway

Slow down and watch for schoolchildren.

Begin slowing down. You must stop soon.

A section of the highway is slippery when wet. Driver should slow down.

Traffic may be moving into your lane. Be ready to change speed or lane.

This means pedestrian crossing. Watch out for people walking across highway.

This means bicycle crossing. Watch out for people riding bicycles.

This sign warns of a hill where driver must take special care.

The unpaved edge of the road is soft. Stay on pavement.

Almost everyone has seen these two warning signs.

This No Passing Zone sign is usually followed by a black and white regulatory sign.

Train may be crossing highway. Slow down and be prepared to stop.

ACTIVITY 2
Identifying warning signs

Match the signs with their meanings.

A.   B.   C.   D.

E.   F.   G.   H.

I.   K.

—— 1. Pedestrian crossing.

—— 2. Watch for bike riders.

—— 3. Watch out for schoolchildren.

—— 4. Highway ahead has two-way traffic.

—— 5. Watch for traffic moving into your lane.

—— 6. Side road ahead—watch for vehicles entering highway.

—— 7. Traffic light ahead. BE PREPARED TO STOP!

—— 8. Railroad Crossing.

—— 9. Curve ahead.

—— 10. Intersection ahead. Watch for vehicles entering, leaving, or crossing highway.

Service and guide signs

Service and guide signs are usually seen on major routes and interstate highways. These signs tell you what to expect ahead. Guide signs are white and green. They point out such things as exits, bike routes, and hiking trails.

They also give distances and directions:

Found above or beside intersections, these signs show the direction to cities.

These signs show distance.

Other signs identify routes by number, symbol, and shape. These routes are part of national, state, and local highway systems.

Interstate sign

U.S. Route markers

A State Highway sign for Michigan

Expressway Exit

On interstate highways and freeways you may see blue-and-white service signs. These signs direct you to rest rooms, telephones, restaurants, and gas stations. Sometimes you will see words and symbols. Sometimes you will see only symbols.

Rest stops

No handicap barriers

Route to nearest hospital

Location of picnic table

Signs showing state and local parks are usually brown with white letters or symbols.

ACTIVITY 3
Identifying street and highway signs

Label these signs as REGULATORY, WARNING, or SERVICE AND GUIDE.

_____

_____

_____

_____

_____

_____

Tell the meaning of each of the following signs.

1. _____

2. _____

3. _____

4. _____

5. _____

6.  _____

7. _____

8. _____

9. _____

10. _____

SHOW WHAT YOU KNOW . . .

About Street and Highway Signs

Working with others in a small group, invent and draw some warning signs and service signs.

HINT: Start with a warning sign for some hazard in your area, such as high waves, air pollution, loud music, skate boarders, or sky divers.

Maps

county route   local road maintained by a county

divided highway   highway that has a strip of grass or concrete between opposite lanes

expressway   divided highway intended for high speeds and having limited entrances and exits

freeway   highway with limited access and without toll charges. Both expressways and freeways usually have two or more lanes in either direction.

grid   system by which points are plotted on a map to help find a location

interchange   place where one or more highways connect. Interchanges usually connect highways intended for high speed.

interstate highway   limited-access federal highway crossing several states

junction   place where two or more roads meet

legend   section of a map where map symbols and signs are explained. Also called a key.

limited-access highway   same as expressway; sometimes called controlled-access highway

points of interest   public places indicated on a map that might be of special interest to travelers. Historic sites and natural features such as waterfalls or rock formations are examples of points of interest.

state highway   highway within a state and maintained wholly or partly by that state

toll road   road on which fees are charged. Fees are also charged on some bridges.

trail   walking or hiking path in a non-urban area. Some highways are called trails.

turnpike   usually refers to a toll road, but some toll-free roads are also called turnpikes

U.S. highway   federal road going across several states but not having controlled access

A map is a drawing that shows some part of the surface of the earth. Maps can show the whole world, a continent, a country, or a state. They can show a county, a city, a town, or a neighborhood. A city map shows streets, neighborhoods, and public buildings. Some city maps show suburbs surrounding a city. Some special maps show rapid transit or bus routes. A map of a park may show trails. Highway maps show roads, highways, and distances between cities. Many maps show natural features, such as rivers, mountains, and lakes. All maps help you find where you are. They also help you get where you're going.

Most maps are drawn so that *north* is at the top of the map. This means that *south* is at the bottom, *east* is at the right, and *west* is at the left. Occasionally, a map will show north slightly to the right or left of the top. A directional symbol on the map will tell you which way is north.

Trail maps   A trail map helps you find your way in a park or wilderness area. Since there are no street signs, only trail markers, you will probably need to carry a trail map when you go to a large park. Study the trail map and the legend below. Notice that each trail is marked with a different symbol.

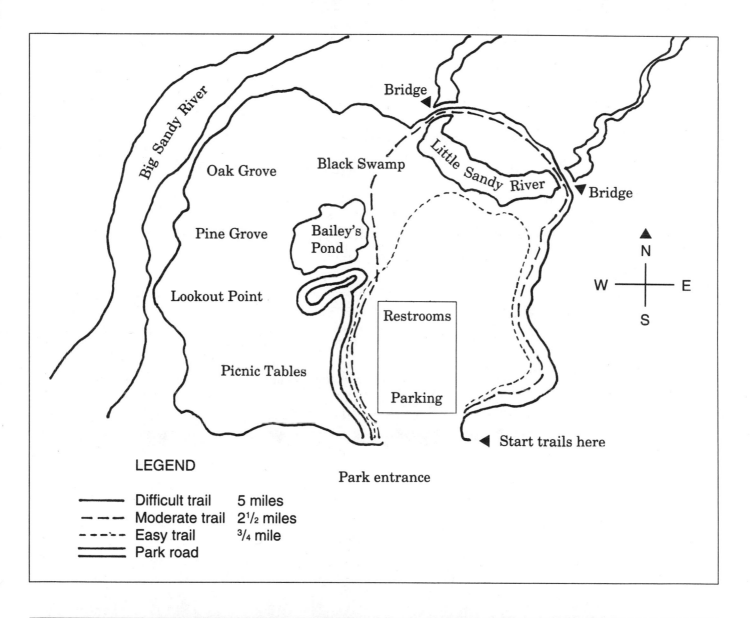

LEGEND

—————— Difficult trail   5 miles
– – – –   Moderate trail   2½ miles
- - - - - Easy trail   ¾ mile
======== Park road

ACTIVITY 4

Understanding a trail map

Use the trail map to answer the questions below.

1. How long is the difficult trail? _____

2. Which trails cross the Little Sandy River? _____

3. Which trail runs closest to Bailey's Pond? _____

4. Can you drive to Bailey's Pond? _____

5. How many trails go to Lookout Point? _____

6. If you are hiking from the second bridge to the Oak Grove, which direction are you going? _____

7. If you are at Lookout Point facing the Big Sandy River at 5 P.M., will the sun be behind you or in front of

   you? _____

8. If you are walking south at the end of the easy trail, will you turn right or left into the parking lot?

   _____

Map legends   A map legend explains the symbols on a map. You used a map legend when you answered the questions about the trail map. On city and highway maps, a map legend will show if you must pay a toll to drive on a road. It will show where you can get on and off a limited-access highway. It will also show a scale of miles. The map legend shown in the next activity also has other information.

ACTIVITY 5
Understanding a map legend

Study this legend from a Wisconsin state map and explain what the following symbols mean.

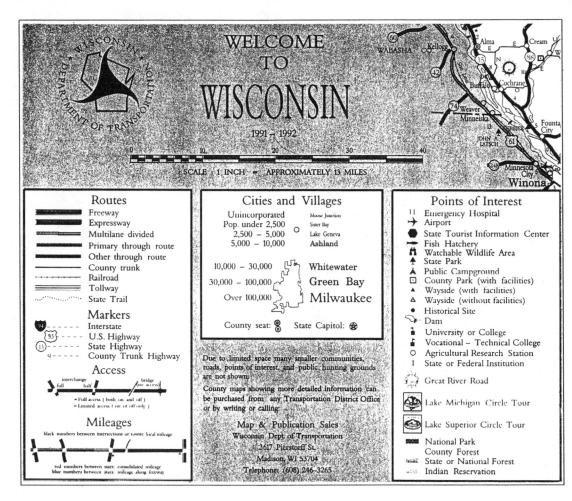

1. ⑬ _____

2. ┼┼┼┼┼ _____

3. 🛡94 _____

4. ⬆ _____

5. ═══ _____

6. 〔53〕 _____

7. ✈ _____

8. ⊙ _____

9. ·········· _____

10. ⬡ _____

Street maps Street maps show the streets in a town or city. Most maps of the downtown area of a city will show all the streets. Some maps of suburban areas show major streets only.

Most street maps show the streets that divide north addresses from south addresses and east from west addresses. For example, there may be an East Washington Street and a West Washington Street. A map will show you where east becomes west.

Streets may be called avenues, boulevards, drives, pikes, places, parkways, trails, and roads. A city may have two streets with almost the same name. For example, there may be a Springfield Road and a Springfield Avenue. There may be an Adams Street and an Adams Parkway. If you are trying to find a certain street, you must know the exact name.

If there are major highways running through a city or town, these will be shown on a city map, too. In addition, some public places may be shown.

In some cities, numbered streets run one direction and non-numbered streets run another. In other cities, streets run in all directions instead of in straight lines. Before you try to find your way, it is a good idea to study a map first.

SHOW WHAT YOU KNOW . . .

About Maps

Draw a map showing the route you take from home to your school. Show major streets and highways only. Include a directional symbol for your map.

ACTIVITY 6

Understanding a street map

Study the map of downtown Detroit. Then answer the questions that follow.

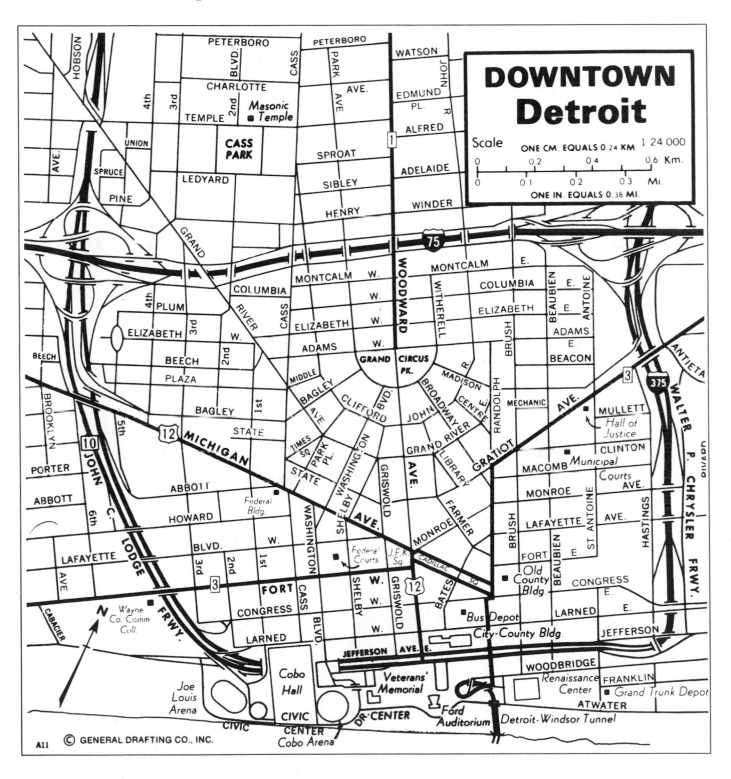

1. Find Grand Circus Park in the middle of the map. Notice that the east-west streets north of the park are named Adams, Elizabeth, Columbia, and so on. What is the dividing street between West Adams and East Adams or between West Elizabeth and East Elizabeth?

   _____

2. Locate Fort Avenue near the bottom of the map. With your finger trace the route to Woodward Avenue (Highway 12) and turn south. Travel Woodward south until you come to Larned Avenue. Turn east and go to Beaubien. Travel north on Beaubien past Macomb and to the corner of Clinton and Beaubien. What public place are you near?

   _____

3. Locate Charlotte Avenue in the upper left portion of the map. Travel east on Charlotte to Cass and turn right. Take Cass to Michigan and travel southeast until you run into Woodward. Take the first right off Woodward to Fort. Take Fort past the John C. Lodge Freeway. Name the educational institution on your left.

   _____

4. You have to meet a friend at the bus depot at the lower right corner of the map between Congress and Larned. If you are coming into the city on the John C. Lodge Freeway, can you exit at Congress?

   _____

5. Is Route 75 an interstate highway or a state highway? _____

6. Look at the scale of kilometers and miles in the upper right-hand corner. Approximately how many kilometers is it from where Route 75 crosses Woodward north to Watson?

   _____

   How many blocks is it? _____

7. Find the directional symbol in the lower left corner of the map. Which way does Michigan Avenue run?

   _____

8. Find Cass Park at the top of the map. Trace the route south on 2nd Blvd. Can you turn right onto Columbia if you are going south?

   _____

Map grids and indexes   A map index and a grid system help you find a place on a map. A map index lists places in alphabetical order. It also lists the *grid points*. A map with grid points usually has letters running vertically on the right side. Numbers run horizontally along the bottom.

```
                          A
                          B
                          C
                          D
                          E
                          F
                          G
        1 2 3 4 5 6 7 8
```

If you want to find a place shown as D–3, run your finger up from 3 and over from D. The location you want should be in that area.

Indexes for cities list streets and public places. Indexes for states list counties and cities.

Here is a map index and a grid for an imaginary place.

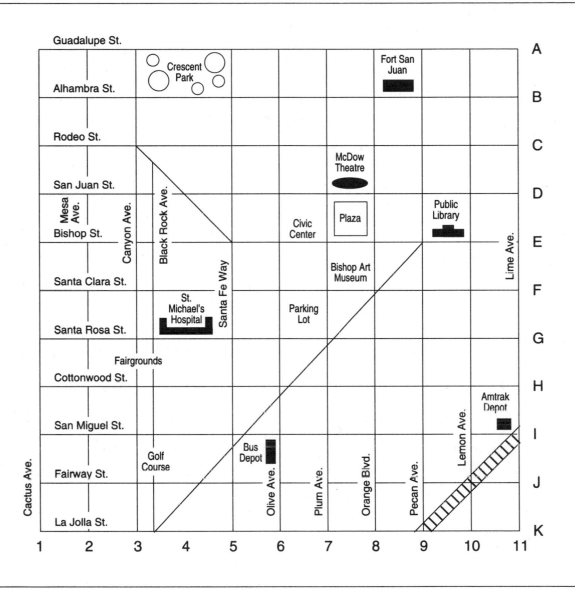

INDEX

Streets

Alhambra B1–B11	Guadalupe A1–A11	Pecan A9–K9
Bishop E1–E11	La Jolla K1–K11	Plum A7–K7
Black Rock D4–K4	Lemon A10–K10	Rodeo C1–C11
Cactus A1–K1	Lime A11–K11	San Juan D1–D11
Canyon C3–K3	Mesa A2–K2	San Miguel I1–I11
Cottonwood H1–H11	Olive A6–K6	Santa Clara F1–F11
El Camino A3–E5	Orange Blvd. A8–K8	Santa Fe Way A5–K5
Firway J1–J11	Orange Pkwy. E9–K4	Santa Rosa G1–G11

Points of Interest

Amtrak Depot I10	McDow Theatre D7–8
Bishop Art Museum E7	Parking Lot F6–7
Bus Depot I6	Public Library E9
Civic Center E6–7	
Crescent Park A3–5	
Fairgrounds G2–4	
Fort San Juan B8–9	
Golf Course I2–3	

ACTIVITY 7
Finding locations with an index and grid

Using the index and grid, answer the following questions.

1. Is Santa Rosa north or south of Bishop? _____

2. What street divides east addresses from west addresses? _____

3. How many blocks away is Plum from Santa Fe Way? _____

4. What are the grid number and letter for the corner of Alhambra Street and Canyon? _____

5. You live on West San Miguel between Mesa and Canyon. How many blocks will you have to walk to the Fairgrounds? _____

6. With the help of the index, find the Bishop Art Museum. Which direction is it from Crescent Park?

_____

7. If you are driving south on El Camino, will you turn right or left to get to the library? _____

8. If you are driving south on Pecan at 7 A.M., will the sun be on your right or your left? _____

9. Orange Boulevard is closed for repairs from Guadalupe to Santa Rosa. Lemon is closed from La Jolla to Cottonwood. How will you get from the Amtrak Station on San Miguel to Fort San Juan?

_____

_____

10. Assume that you have a friend who lives at C–3. What streets intersect at this junction?

_____

State highway maps

Highway maps are important for travelers. Truck drivers need them, bus drivers need them, and tourists need them. State maps show many kinds of highways. Even-numbered highways run generally east and west. Odd-numbered highways run generally north and south.

ACTIVITY 8
Understanding a state highway map

Study the map of the southeast part of Wisconsin to answer the questions. The legend for the map is on page 31.

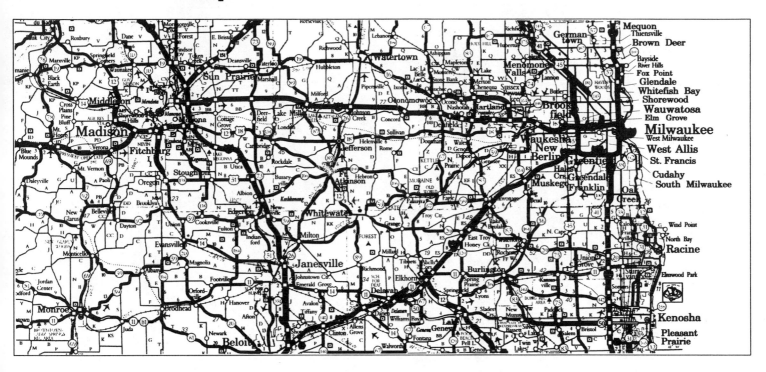

1. What highway will you take from Madison to Milwaukee if you are in a hurry? _____

2. What highway might you take from Madison to Milwaukee if you want to travel more slowly?

   _____

3. Locate two state parks in the southeast area of the map.

   Write their names here. _____

4. What is the name of the state forest west of Milwaukee? _____

5. Can you camp in this forest? _____

6. Racine and Kenosha are south of Milwaukee on Lake Michigan. Are they county seats? _____

7. Highway 90 goes from Madison southeast to Janesville. Can you get off 90 at route 26? _____

8. Find Beloit at the bottom of the map. If you take route 213 northwest out of Beloit, what is the first

   town you come to? What is the next town on route 213? _____

9. Continue on route 213. Is Evansville a bigger or smaller town than Beloit? _____

10. Is there an airport near Janesville? _____

Study this map of Baltimore, Maryland. Answer the questions about it.

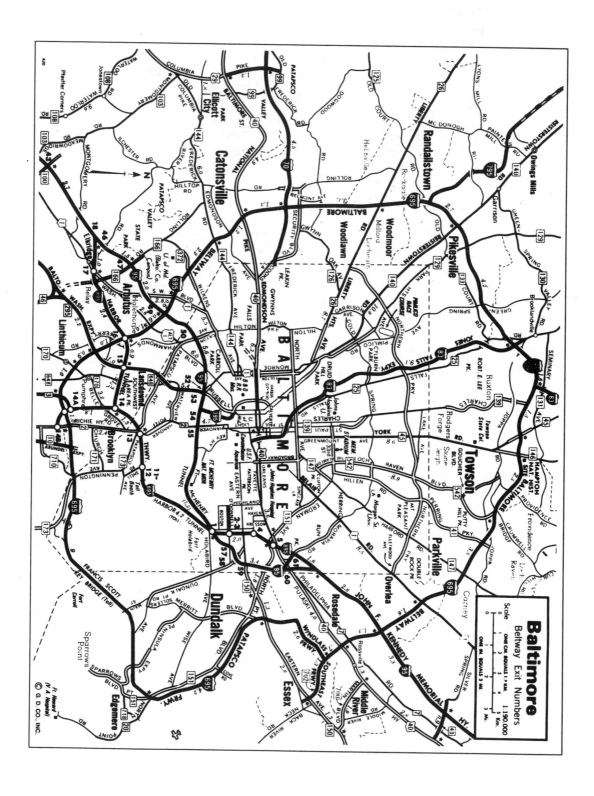

1. Which interstate route goes to the center of Baltimore? _____

2. Which highway is named after John F. Kennedy? _____

3. What are two ways to get from Dundalk to Brooklyn? _____

_____

4. Is the Pimlico Race Course southeast or northwest of Pikesville? _____

5. What highway is also called the Baltimore Beltway? _____

6. What state park is in the southwest corner of the map? _____

_____

7. What is the most direct route from Arbutus to downtown Baltimore? _____

_____

8. Does this map show all the streets in Baltimore or just major routes? _____

_____

SHOW WHAT YOU KNOW . . .

About Mapping a Route

Using a road atlas that has a map of the whole United States, find the state where you live. Trace the route you would take to the nation's capital. If you live in or near Washington, D.C., trace the route you would take to get to St. Louis, Missouri. If you do not own the atlas you are using, photocopy the map first for this activity.

Timetables

WORDS TO KNOW

A.M. from midnight to noon (morning)

arrival time the expected time you will get where you are going

departure time the time of leaving

originating point the place a trip starts

P.M. from noon to midnight (afternoon and evening)

terminating point the place a trip ends (last stop on bus, boat, train, or plane)

timetable schedule that shows the times when planes, trains, and so on arrive and depart

What time will your train leave Charleston, West Virginia, for Washington, D.C.? Is there a morning bus to Hillside, New Jersey? Are there any evening flights from Chicago to Denver? When does the last ferry boat leave Mackinac Island?

Being able to read a schedule or timetable can come in very handy. Timetables can help you get to work on time. They can make travel and vacations easier. They can help you plan your time. They can help keep you from being in the wrong place at the wrong time. Timetables tell you when you'll get where you are going. Some timetables tell you all the stops along the way. Before you take a bus, train, boat, or plane, you should know how to read a timetable.

Reading timetables

All timetables show the starting or originating point and the ending or terminating point.

The bus timetable below shows only two points—originating and terminating. But some timetables show all points between these locations. These points are called stops.

All timetables show departure times and arrival times.

Most timetables are read either down or across. This means that you may read across the schedule to locate your arrival time. Or you may read down the schedule to locate your arrival time. When there is only one place of departure and arrival, timetables usually read *across*.

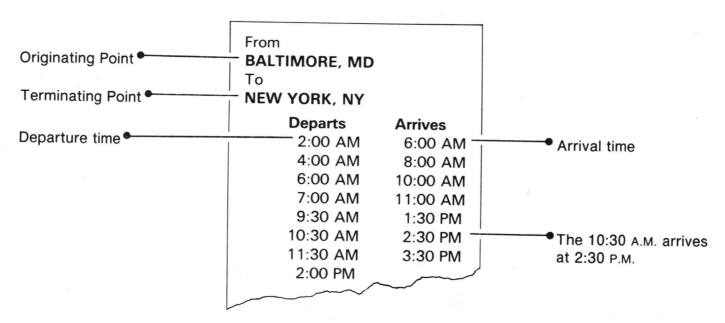

In the sample above, the column headings help you read this timetable. First you read your departure time under "Departs." Then you read across the same line. You locate your arrival time under "Arrives." Many transportation schedules have several columns. They also show many stops. You must study these timetables to determine how you should read them.

In the next schedule there are five columns showing departures. These show buses going from Baltimore to New York. These are buses #1, #2, #3, #4, and #5. They all make the same run. This schedule reads *down*.

Read down
from Baltimore
to New York ●——————

Bus #3
Leaves at
12:00 noon ●——

Arrives at ●——
4:30 P.M.

From **BALTIMORE, MD** To **NEW YORK, NY**	#1 Sun	#2	#3	#4	#5
Baltimore, MD	9:00	8:00	**12:00**	**6:00**	2:00
Joppatowne, MD	—	8:15	**12:15**	**6:15**	2:15
Edgewood, MD	—	8:30	**12:30**	**6:30**	2:30
Aberdeen, MD	—	8:45	**12:45**	**6:45**	2:45
Havre de Grace, MD	—	9:00	**1:00**	**7:00**	3:00
Elkton, MD	—	9:30	**1:30**	**7:30**	3:30
Wilmington, DE	10:45	9:45	**1:45**	**7:45**	3:45
Newark, NJ	**1:00**	**12:00**	**4:00**	**10:00**	6:00
New York City	**1:30**	**12:30**	**4:30**	**10:30**	6:30

Notes:
P.M.—Boldface   All trips operate daily
Sun—Sundays only   unless otherwise noted.

Reading down, Bus #3 leaves Baltimore at 12:00 noon. It goes through Joppatowne, Edgewood, and so on until it arrives in New York City at 4:30 P.M. If you want to leave at 2:00 A.M., you locate the 2:00 A.M. bus (#5). You then read down to your destination for the arrival time. At the bottom of a schedule is a "notes" section. Abbreviations and symbols used are explained here. On many transportation timetables this section is called the "key." Look at the "notes" section of this timetable.

The "notes" section tells you that buses that run between 12 noon and midnight are shown in boldface (dark) type. The symbols A.M. and P.M. do not appear on the timetable. You must read the notes in order to get the correct time for the bus you want to take. Also notice that bus #1 runs only on Sundays. It is possible to travel from Baltimore to New York City by bus on Sunday, but you must take the 9 A.M. bus. There are no other buses that day from Baltimore to New York City.

ACTIVITY 9
Understanding timetables

The timetable below shows trains going from New York City to Detroit. You have to read *down* this schedule to find stops (and departure times) between these two cities.

New York-Albany-Syracuse- Rochester-Buffalo-Niagara Falls-Detroit

Km	Mi			63	69	73	71	75	65	49	79
		Train Name		The Niagara Rainbow	The Adirondack	The Empire State Express	The Henry Hudson	The Washington Irving	The Salt City Express	The Lake Shore Limited	The DeWitt Clinton
		Frequency of Operation		Daily	Daily	Daily	Daily	Daily	Daily	Daily	Daily
		Type of Service		⊠ ▭	⊠	✓ ⊠	⊠	⊠	✓ ⊠	⇌ ✕ ▭	⊠
0	0	*(Conrail)* **New York, NY** *(ET)* *(Grand Central Terminal)*	Dp	8 40 A	9 15 A	12 40 P	2 40 P	4 40 P	5 40 P	6 40 P	8 40 P
53	33	Croton-Harmon, NY ⑯		R 9 37 A	R 10 03 A	R 1 28 P	R 3 28 P	R 5 28 P	R 6 28 P	R 7 37 P	R 9 28 P
119	74	Poughkeepsie, NY ⑲ *(Highland)*		R 10 21 A	R 10 48 A	R 2 13 P	R 4 13 P	R 6 13 P	R 7 13 P	R 8 21 P	R 10 13 P
143	89	Rhinecliff, NY *(Kingston)*		10 37 A	11 04 A	2 29 P	4 29 P	6 29 P	7 29 P	8 37 P	10 29 P
185	115	Hudson, NY		11 02 A	11 27 A	2 52 P	4 52 P	6 52 P	7 52 P	9 02 P	10 52 P
230	143	**Albany-Rensselaer, NY**	Ar	11 45 A	12 05 P	3 30 P	5 30 P	7 30 P	8 30 P	9 45 P	11 30 P
230	143		Dp	12 05 P		3 40 P			8 40 P	10 00 P	
245	152	Colonie-Schenectady, NY		12 26 P		3 55 P			8 55 P		
257	160	Schenectady, NY		㉖		㉖			㉖	㉖	
286	178	Amsterdam, NY		12 54 P		4 20 P			9 20 P		
383	238	**Utica, NY**		1 55 P		5 17 P			10 17 P	11 52 P	
406	252	Rome, NY *(Griffiss AFB)*		2 11 P		5 31 P			10 31 P		
460	286	**Syracuse, NY**		2 42 P		6 02 P			11 05 P	12 45 A	
599	372	**Rochester, NY**		4 15 P		7 32 P				2 20 A	
695	432	Cheektowaga, NY ㉖ ●									
705	438	Buffalo, NY *(Central Tml.)*		5 32 P		8 40 P				3 50 A	
708	440	**Buffalo, NY** *(Exchange St.)*	Ar	5 37 P		8 45 P					
748	465	**Niagara Falls, NY**		6 40 P		9 45 P					
938	583	St. Thomas, Ont. ●		9 28 P							
1115	693	Windsor, Ont. ● *(Amtrak Sta.)*		11 10 P							
1120	696	**Detroit, MI** *(Amtrak Sta.) (ET)*	Ar	11 30 P							

Answer these questions about the train schedule above.

1. How many trains appear on this schedule? _____

2. What is the distance between New York City and Rochester? _____

3. What is the number of the train that goes all the way from New York City to Detroit? _____

4. If you want to be in Utica by 3 P.M., which train will you take? _____

5. What time does this train leave New York City? _____

6. What time does this train arrive in Detroit? _____

7. What is the last stop for the Henry Hudson? _____

8. What time does the Adirondack get to Hudson? _____

9. What time does the Washington Irving leave New York City? _____

10. Does the Lake Shore Limited leave New York City in the morning or evening? _____

ACTIVITY 10
Understanding timetables

As you read *across* the airline schedule on the next page, each column gives you information on a specific flight. (The codes and abbreviations used here would be explained at the bottom of the schedule.) You learn when a flight leaves and when a flight arrives. You learn a flight's number and how often a plane flies. Continuing to read across, you will find a column for connecting cities and one showing the stops a plane makes. Use this schedule to answer the questions below.

1. Determine the departure time, the arrival time, and the number of stops for each of these Asheville flights:

FROM ASHEVILLE, N.C.

TO

	Flight #	Departure Time	Arrival Time	# of Stops
Augusta, Ga.	88/918			
Charleston, W. Va.	60			
Columbia, S.C.	88/918			

2. How many flights leave Asheville each day for

Atlanta, Ga.? _____

Chicago, Ill.? _____

Columbus, Ohio? _____

3. If you leave for Atlanta, Ga., at 9:52, you will be on what flight? _____

4. If you leave Asheville for Augusta, in what city will you have to make a connection? _____

5. What will be your flight number when you leave the connecting city for Columbus, Ohio? _____

6. Name at least four cities to which this airline has nonstop flights. _____

_____

_____

7. Flight #62 from Asheville to Fayetteville/Fort Bragg, N.C., operates daily except _____ .

8. Which flight makes the most stops? _____

• Column 1–*Leave* = Time plane leaves Asheville, N.C.

• Column 2–*Arrive* = Time plane arrives in desired city

• Column 3–*Flight No.* = Number identifying a particular flight

1	2	3	4	5	6
Leave	Arrive	Flight-No.	Freq.	Connect Via	Stops

FROM ASHEVILLE, N. C.

Leave	Arrive	Flight-No.	Freq.	Connect Via	Stops
Reservations				254-4621	
TO					
ATLANTA, GA.					
8 30a	9 12a	43			0
9 52a	10 48a	943			0
1 35p	2 15p	47			0
4 25p	5 07p	88			0
9 35p	10 15p	39			0
AUGUSTA, GA.					
$ 9 52a	12 50p	943/914		Atlanta	1
$ 4 25p	6 25p	88/918	Ex Sa	Atlanta	1
$ 4 25p	6 25p	88/926	Sa Only	Atlanta	1
CHARLESTON, W. VA.					
8 10a	8 52a	60			0
CHARLOTTE, N. C.					
5 44p	6 15p	960			0
CHICAGO, ILL.					
$ 8 10a	11 39a ⊚	60/67		Charleston	2
$ 11 30a	12 38p ⊚	89			1
$ 2 30p	6 47p ⊚	10/81		Roanoke	2
CINCINNATI, OHIO					
$ 5 30p	9 46p	24/927		Winston-Salem	4
COLUMBIA, S. C.					
$ 4 25p	7 01p	88/918	Ex Sa	Atlanta	2
$ 4 25p	7 01p	88/926	Sa Only	Atlanta	2
COLUMBUS, OHIO					
8 10a	12 17p	60/951		Charleston	2
FAYETTEVILLE/FORT BRAGG, N. C.					
8 02a	9 14a	72			1
10 30p	11 10p	62	Ex Sa		0
GREENVILLE/SPARTANBURG, S. C.					
8 02a	8 23a	72			0
HICKORY/LENOIR/MORGANTON, N. C.					
7 34p	7 59p	922			0
HUNTINGTON, W. VA./ASHLAND, KY./IRONTON, OHIO					
8 10a	11 10a	60/67		Charleston	1
KINSTON/GOLDSBORO/GREENVILLE/CAMP LEJEUNE, N. C.					
5 44p	8 47p	960/964		Raleigh	2
KNOXVILLE/OAK RIDGE, TENN.					
11 14a	11 46a	969			0

Column 4–*Freq.* = Whether or not flights are daily. *Exceptions* appear here

Column 5–*Connect Via* = Name of the connect city, when you have to change planes

Column 6–*Stops* = Number of stops between "Leave" and "Arrive"

ACTIVITY 11
Reading an airport terminal schedule

Airports post arrival and departure information. They show flight numbers. They also show departure and arrival times for these flights. This information usually appears on a screen or board. Some airports show destinations and gate numbers. They may also show whether a plane is delayed, on time, or boarding.

ARRIVALS				
Time	Flight #	Gate	From	Comments
2:15	72	7	Detroit	Arrived
2:20	174	9	Chicago	Landing
2:45	49	10	Houston	On Time
2:50	74	6	Dallas	On Time
3:00	711	5	Los Angeles	Delayed
3:10	80	4	Roanoke	On Time
3:15	39	3	Houston	On Time
3:20	63	2	Boston	On Time
		TIME 2:17		

DEPARTURES				
Time	Flight #	Gate	To	Comments
3:10	71	33	Cleveland	Boarding
3:20	412	36	Boston	On Time
3:30	576	34	San Francisco	On Time
3:45	232	35	Dallas/Ft. Worth	On Time
4:00	109	39	Chicago	On Time
4:10	57	41	Detroit	On Time
4:15	74	32	Memphis	Delayed
		TIME 3:06		

Answer these questions about the schedules above.

1. What time is flight 80 scheduled to arrive? _____ Will it be on time? _____

2. What time is flight 711 scheduled to arrive? _____ Will it be on time? _____

3. Which flight arrives at Gate 10? _____ Gate 6? _____ Gate 3? _____

4. You have to meet a friend arriving from Chicago at 2:20. It is 2:17. Is the plane at the gate?

_____

45

5. What time is flight 74 scheduled to leave for Memphis? _____

   Will it leave on time? _____

6. Is flight 71 to Cleveland delayed? _____

7. Are passengers boarding flight 71 to Cleveland? If so, what gate are they using? _____

8. What is the flight number of the 3:20 flight to Boston? _____

9. Where is flight 57 scheduled to go? _____

ACTIVITY 12
Understanding timetables

Some timetables must be read down one side and up the other. The names of the stops are centered. Schedule information is on both sides.

In this timetable you read down to find departure times for buses going in one direction (Ocean City, Md.) You read up the opposite side to find departure times for buses going in the opposite direction (Philadelphia, Pa.). Like all transportation timetables, this timetable shows arrival and departure times as either A.M. or P.M. In this timetable, A.M. is in lightface type, P.M. is in boldface (heavier) type. Other special information is explained at the bottom of the timetable.

Answer the questions about this interstate bus timetable.

NEW YORK PHILADELPHIA REHOBOTH BEACH OCEAN CITY

READ DOWN		No. **7303** 9-21-81	No. POC	READ UP
---- ---- ----	5 30 2 00	Lv **Philadelphia, PA** ♦ CCC	Ar 1135	3 35 7 35 ----
---- ---- ----	6 05 2 30	Chester, PA ♦ (7300)	1100	3 00 7 00 ----
---- ---- ----	6 35 3 00	**Wilmington, DE** 318 N. Market	1035	2 35 6 35 ----
---- ---- ----	6 50 3 15	Ar State Road, DE CCC	Lv 1020	2 20 6 20 ----
---- ---- ----	3 00 1 00	Lv NEW YORK, NY (7909)**TWI**	Ar 1 00	4 50 8 35 ----
---- ---- ----	6 50 3 25	Ar State Road, DE (7909)**TWI**	Lv 1010	2 25 6 10 ----
---- ---- ----	7 05 3 35	Lv State Road, DE	Ar 1005	2 05 5 55 ----
---- ---- ----	7 40 d	Smyrna	9 28	ss 5 32 ----
---- ---- ----	8 00 4 25	**Dover**	9 10	1 15 5 00 ----
---- ---- ----	8 25 4 55	Ar Harrington (7300)	Lv 8 40	12ᵇ45 4 30 ----
---- ---- ----	8ᵇ25 4 55	Lv Harrington (7301)	Ar 8 40	12 40 4 30 ----
---- ---- ----	8 40	Ar Milford (7300)	Lv	12 25 4 35 ----
---- ---- ----	8 40	Lv Milford (7301)	Ar	12 25 4 35 ----
---- ---- ----	d	Lewes		11 40 ----
---- ---- ----	9 25	Ar **Rehoboth Beach**	Lv	11 30 ----
---- ---- ----	9 45	Bethany Beach, DE		11 05 ----
---- ---- ----	5 55	Ar Salisbury, MD (7300)	Lv 7 40	3ᵇ35 ----
---- ---- ----	6ᵇ00	Lv Salisbury, MD (7301)	Ar 7 35	3 25 ----
---- ---- ----	1005 6 50	Ar **Ocean City, MD** CCC	Lv 6 45	10 45 2 45 ----
		Mi.	Mi.	

Reference Marks for Tables 7301, 7303 and 7307

X—No local passengers carried between these points.

All trips operate daily unless otherwise noted.
AM—Light Face. **PM—Bold Face.**
Times shown in ITALICS indicate service via connecting trip or trips.

Sun—Sundays only.
Fri—Fridays only.
hs—Highway stop.
f—Flag stop.
d—Discharge passengers only.
N—No interstate service.
♦—Interstate service only.
POC—Thru Philadelphia–Ocean City.

B—Via Baltimore.
ss—Station stop.
OC—On Call.

1. This timetable shows buses connecting what two main points? _____

2. If you were traveling from Chester, Pa., to Ocean City, Md., would you read *up* or *down* the schedule?

3. If you were traveling from Ocean City, Md., to Chester, Pa., would you read *up* or *down* the schedule? _____

4. What time does the bus that leaves Philadelphia at 5:30 arrive in Ocean City? _____

5. What time is this bus scheduled to leave Chester, Pa.? _____
   Wilmington, Del.? _____

6. What time is this bus scheduled to arrive at Delaware (State Road stop)? _____
   Harrington, Del.? _____
   Milford, Del.? _____

7. If you left New York City at 3:00 in the afternoon, at what stop would you connect with the bus going to Ocean City? _____

8. List all the stops the 2:45 Ocean City bus makes before it gets to State Road.
   1st STOP _____
   2nd STOP _____
   3rd STOP _____
   4th STOP _____
   5th STOP _____

9. If you left New York City on the 1:00 bus, what time would you arrive at the State Road stop in Delaware? _____

10. What time does the 5:30 bus out of Philadelphia arrive at the State Road stop in Delaware?
   _____

The timetable below shows the train going from Salt Lake City to Seattle. And it shows the train from Seattle to Salt Lake City. You read down the left side of the schedule to find departure times for trains going to Seattle. These trains are traveling westward. You read up the opposite side of the schedule to find departure times for trains going to Salt Lake City. These trains are traveling eastward.

The Pioneer

Salt Lake City
Ogden
Boise
Portland
Seattle

READ DOWN						READ UP
25			Train Number			26
Daily			Frequency of Operation			Daily
🛏 ⊠ ▢			Type of Service			🛏 ⊠ ▢
	Km	Mi	*(Union Pacific)*			
11 25 P	0	0	Dp **Salt Lake City, UT** *(Amtrak Sta.) (MT)* Ar			7 10 A
12 20 A	58	36	Ar **Ogden, UT**	Dp		6 10 A
12 35 A	58	36	Dp	Ar		5 55 A
F 1 05 A	92	57	Brigham City, UT ●			F 5 25 A
3 20 A	276	170	Ar **Pocatello, ID**	Dp		3 10 A
3 30 A	276	170	Dp	Ar		3 00 A
5 15 A	447	278	Shoshone, ID ●			1 10 A
F 6 30 A	576	358	Mountain Home, ID ●			F 11 55 P
7 30 A	650	404	**Boise, ID**			10 50 P
8 10 A	682	424	Nampa, ID ● *(Caldwell)*			10 10 P
8 50 A	750	466	Ontario, OR ● *(MT)*			9 30 P
9 50 A	890	553	Baker, OR ● *(PT)*			6 30 P
11 10 A	975	606	La Grande, OR ●			5 30 P
1 30 P	1094	680	Pendleton, OR ●			3 10 P
2 05 P	1144	711	Hinkle, OR ● *(Hermiston)*			2 35 P
3 35 P	1302	809	The Dalles, OR ●			1 00 P
F 4 10 P	1339	832	Hood River, OR ●			F 12 30 P
5 50 P	1440	895	Ar **Portland, OR**	Dp		11 10 A
6 00 P	1440	895	Dp	Ar		11 00 A
			(Burlington Northern)			
6 21 P	1456	905	Vancouver, WA			10 33 A
7 00 P	1519	944	Kelso-Longview, WA			9 55 A
7 45 P	1588	987	Centralia, WA			9 06 A
8 05 P	1619	1006	East Olympia, WA ●			8 46 A
8 50 P	1675	1041	Tacoma, WA			8 06 A
9 50 P	1740	1081	Ar **Seattle, WA** *(King St. Sta.) (PT)*	Dp		7 10 A

The Pioneer
Salt Lake City-Seattle   **Services**   Amfleet Service
Tray Meal and Beverage Service—*Am-dinette*
Sleeping Car Service—Complimentary coffee and tea served on request 6:30-9:30 AM.
Coach Service—Reserved and unreserved seats.
Baggage Service—Checked baggage handled at Ogden, Pocatello, Boise, Portland and Seattle.

Answer these questions about this timetable. Read *down* the schedule.

1. What is the name of this train? _____

2. What is the number of this train when it is going from Salt Lake City to Seattle? _____

Seattle to Salt Lake City? _____

3. What time does this train leave Salt Lake City for Seattle? _____

4. What time does this train arrive in Ogden? _____

5. What time does it leave Ogden? _____

6. What time does this train leave La Grande, Ore.? _____ Pendleton, Ore.? _____

Portland, Ore.? _____ Vancouver, Wash.? _____

7. What time is the train scheduled to arrive in Seattle? _____

Answer these questions about this timetable. This time read *up* the schedule.

1. What time does the train leave Seattle for Salt Lake City? _____

2. What is the first stop after Seattle? _____

3. What time does the train arrive in Portland? _____

4. What time does it leave Portland? _____

5. What is the stop before Nampa, Idaho? _____

6. What time is this train due to arrive in Salt Lake City? _____

SHOW WHAT YOU KNOW . . .

About Timetables

According to the timetable on page 48, how many hours does it take the *Pioneer* to go from Salt Lake City to Seattle? How many miles is it? Figure out how many miles an hour the train travels on the average.

Charts and graphs

Charts   Some information can be found and understood more quickly if it appears in a chart or graph. It is often easier to see how one set of information changes or depends on another. A chart lists information. It also helps you make comparisons.

ANNUAL FUEL COSTS CHART

Dollars Per Gallon

ESTIMATED MPG	1.40	1.30	1.20	1.10	1.00	0.90	0.80
50	$420	$390	$360	$330	$300	$270	$240
49	428	398	367	337	304	275	245
48	437	406	374	343	312	281	250
47	447	415	383	351	320	288	256
46	456	423	391	358	326	293	260
45	466	433	400	366	333	300	266
44	477	443	409	375	340	306	272
43	489	454	419	384	350	315	280
42	500	464	428	393	357	321	286
41	512	476	439	403	366	329	293
40	525	488	450	412	375	338	300
39	538	499	461	422	384	346	307
38	552	513	473	434	394	355	316
37	567	526	486	446	405	364	324
36	584	542	500	459	417	375	334
35	601	558	515	472	429	386	343
34	617	573	529	485	441	397	353
33	636	591	545	500	454	409	364
32	655	608	562	515	468	421	374
31	678	630	581	533	484	436	388
30	699	649	599	549	500	450	400
29	724	673	621	569	518	466	414
28	750	696	643	589	536	482	428
27	777	722	666	610	555	500	444
26	808	751	693	635	578	520	462
25	840	780	720	660	600	540	480
24	876	813	751	688	626	563	500
23	914	848	783	718	652	587	522
22	956	887	819	751	682	614	546
21	1000	928	857	785	714	643	571
20	1050	975	900	825	750	675	600
19	1105	1026	947	868	789	710	631
18	1168	1084	1001	917	834	751	667
17	1235	1147	1058	970	882	794	706
16	1312	1219	1125	1031	938	844	750
15	1401	1301	1201	1101	1000	900	800
14	1499	1392	1285	1178	1071	964	857
13	1615	1500	1384	1269	1154	1038	923
12	1749	1624	1499	1374	1250	1125	1000
11	1909	1773	1636	1500	1364	1227	1091
10	2100	1950	1800	1630	1500	1350	1200
9	2333	2166	2000	1833	1666	1500	1333
8	2625	2438	2250	2062	1875	1688	1500
7	3001	2787	2572	2358	2144	1929	1715
6	3501	3251	3031	2751	2500	2250	2000
5	4200	3900	3600	3300	3000	2700	2400

The chart shows annual fuel costs. Different cars get different gas mileage. This chart shows the cost of gasoline for one year. It shows this based on the average number of miles a car gets per gallon of gas. The miles per gallon (MPG) are shown vertically. They are on the left side of the chart. The cost of gasoline is shown horizontally. "Dollars Per Gallon" appears across the top of the chart. Let's say your car gets about 36 miles to a gallon. You locate "36" in the vertical column labeled ESTIMATED MPG. Then you read across the top of the chart. You find what you pay for gasoline. If you pay $1.30 per gallon, your annual fuel cost is $542.

ACTIVITY 13
Reading a temperature chart

Below is a temperature chart. It gives the average high and low Farenheit temperatures for three states. They are Georgia, North Carolina, and South Carolina. Study the chart. Then answer the questions.

Note: Maximum temperatures appear above the line. Minimum temperatures appear below the line.

Temperature Averages - Maximum/Minimum From the records of the National Weather Service												
	JAN.	FEB.	MAR.	APR.	MAY	JUNE	JULY	AUG.	SEPT.	OCT.	NOV.	DEC.
GEORGIA												
Atlanta	54/36	57/37	63/41	72/50	81/59	87/66	88/69	88/68	83/63	74/52	62/40	53/35
Augusta	59/36	62/37	67/43	77/50	84/59	91/67	91/70	91/69	87/64	78/52	68/40	59/35
Columbus	59/37	61/38	67/43	76/51	85/60	91/68	92/71	91/70	87/65	78/53	67/42	59/36
Macon	60/38	63/39	69/45	78/53	87/61	93/69	93/71	92/70	88/65	79/54	68/43	60/38
Savannah	63/41	64/42	70/47	77/54	85/62	90/69	91/71	91/71	86/67	78/56	69/46	63/40
NORTH CAROLINA												
Asheville	49/30	51/31	57/36	68/44	76/53	83/60	85/64	74/63	79/57	69/46	57/36	50/30
Cape Hatteras	52/40	54/40	58/44	66/52	75/61	82/69	84/72	84/72	80/68	71/59	63/50	55/42
Charlotte	53/33	56/34	62/39	72/49	80/58	88/66	89/69	88/68	83/62	74/50	63/39	53/33
Raleigh	52/31	54/32	61/38	72/47	79/56	86/64	87/68	88/67	82/60	73/48	62/38	52/31
Winston-Salem	50/32	52/32	59/37	70/47	79/56	87/65	88/68	87/67	81/62	72/49	60/38	50/32
SOUTH CAROLINA												
Charleston	59/44	60/44	65/50	73/58	81/66	86/73	88/75	82/75	83/70	75/61	66/50	59/44
Columbia	58/36	61/36	67/42	76/51	85/60	92/70	93/71	92/70	86/65	77/52	67/41	58/35
Florence	58/37	60/37	67/43	76/51	84/60	90/68	91/70	90/70	85/64	77/53	67/43	58/36
Spartanburg	53/35	55/35	62/40	72/50	81/59	88/67	89/69	88/68	82/63	73/52	62/41	53/34

1. What is the maximum average temperature in Atlanta, Georgia, in January? _____

2. What is the minimum average temperature in Atlanta, Georgia, in January? _____

3. What is the maximum average temperature in Macon, Georgia, in July? _____

4. During which month does Columbus, Georgia, have its lowest temperature? _____

5. During which month does Raleigh, North Carolina, have its highest temperature? _____

6. Which city has the highest temperature in August—Charleston or Florence? _____

7. Which city has the lowest temperature in January? _____

8. Which city has the highest temperature in January? _____

ACTIVITY 14
Reading a recreation site chart

Use this chart of recreation areas to answer the questions below.

Facilities \ Parks	Audra	Babcock	Beartown	Beech Fork	Berkeley Spr.	Blackwater Falls	Bluestone	Cacapon	Canaan Valley	Carnifax Ferry Battlefield	Cass Scenic R.R.	Cathedral	Cedar Creek	Chief Logan	Droop Mountain Battlefield	Fairfax Stone	Grandview	Greenbrier River Trail	Hawks Nest	Holly River	Little Beaver	Lost River	North Bend	Pinnacle Rock	Pipestem	Prickets Fort	Pt. Pleasant Monument	Tomlinson Run	Twin Falls	Tygart Lake	Valley Falls	Watoga	Watters Smith Mem.	Cabwaylingo	Cal Price	Camp Creek	Coopers Rock	Greenbrier	Kanawha	Kumbrabow	Panther	Seneca
Deluxe Cabins					25	25	11	15													9	8			25				13	10		8										
Standard Cabins		18						13			5										9	15							25			13				12						
Economy Cabins		8						6																																		
Rustic Cabins																																									5	7
Lodge Rooms					55			50	250										31				30		143				20	20												
Tent/Trailer Sites	65	50		275		65	87		34	N	N		46						88		N	55			50			50	50	40		88		34		12	24	16	46	7	6	10
Restaurant		■			■	■	■	■		N			■						■	■			■	■	■				■	■		■		N					N			
Refreshments	■	■		N	■	■	■	■	■	N		■	■		■			■	■	■			■	■	■			■	■	■		■					■	■	■		■	
Groceries	N	■			N	■	N	N		N			■	N				■	■	N	■	N	■		■					■		N		N				N	N			N
Golf Course		N			N	N	■	■															■		■			■	■	N		N							N			
Swimming	S	P			P	L	P	L	P				P	P					P	P			P	P	P			P	P	L		P	P	P			P		P	P	P	P
Boat Rental		■				■	■	■											■		■				N			■		■		■		■								
Boat Launch Ramp			■			■													■						N	■				■												
Fishing		■		N	■	■	■			■	■						N	■	■				■		■			■	■	■		■		■	■	■	■	■	N		■	■	■
Rental Horses		■				■		■	N												■		■						■	■												
Picnicking	■	■	■		■	■	■	■		■	■	■	■	■		■		■	■	■	■	■	■	■	■			■	■	■		■	■	■		■	■	■	■	■	■	■
Game Courts		■			■	■	■	■	■				■	■					■		■				■			■	■	■		■					■					
Playgrounds	■	■			■	■	■	■		■	■	■	■				■		■				■		■			■	■	■		■		■			■		■	■	■	■
Hiking Trails	■	■	■	■	■	■	■	■	■		■	■	■	■		■	■	■	■	■	■		■		■			■	■	■	■	■	■	■		■	■	■	■	■	■	■
Natural Interest		■				■							■				■									■			■	■		■										
Naturalist		■		■	■	■	■	■									■		■	■			■					■	■	■		■										
Museum							■	N					■			■			■				■			■	■	■				■										
Historical Interest						■					■	■			■	■			■				■			■	■	■				■						■				
Souvenir Shop		■				■			■	■	N							■	■	■			■	■	■				■	■		■	■					■				
Map Reference	F4	E7	F6	B6	J3	H4	E7	J3	H4	E6	G6	G4	E5	B7	F6	H4	D7	F7	D6	F5	D7	I5	D4	D8	D7	F4	B5	E1	D7	F4	F4	F6	F4	B7	F6	D7	G3	F7	C6	F5	C8	G6

N-nearby   P-pool   L-lake   S-stream

1. If you want to know which parks have a particular feature (for example, hiking trails), would you read *down* this chart or *across*? _____

2. If you want to know which features a particular park has (for example, Bluestone), would you read *down* this chart or *across*? _____

3. Does Grandview have cabins? _____

4. List the parks with boat ramps. _____

_____

5. Which parks have lakes? _____

_____

6. How is a "nearby" facility shown on this chart? _____

Graphs Graphs give information, too. Look at the graph below. It shows the annual attendance at the local zoo.

ATTENDANCE AT LOCAL ZOO

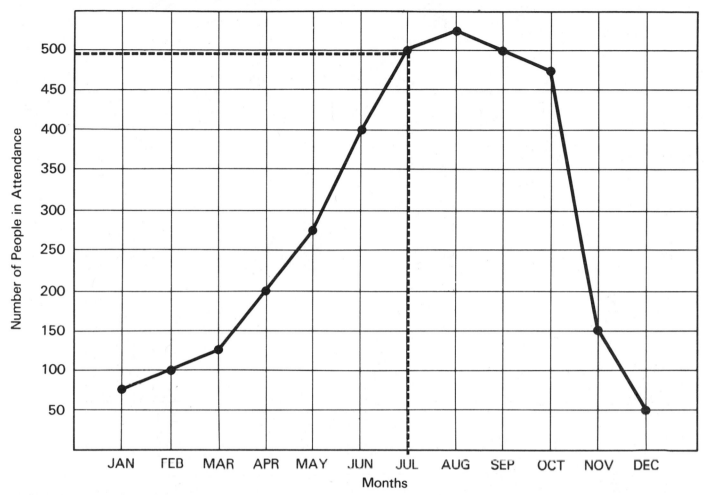

The vertical axis shows the number of people in attendance. It is divided into units of 50 through 500. The horizontal axis shows the months of the year. You plot information on the graph. You do this by locating the point where the horizontal and vertical lines meet. The horizontal point shows the month. The vertical point shows the number of people at the zoo. In July there were 500 people in attendance at the local zoo.

You form the lines on the graph by connecting the dots. Each dot represents attendance for a given month. This type of graph is a line graph.

ACTIVITY 15
Reading a line graph

How did the track team do with its potato chip sales? How many cases of popcorn did the cheerleaders sell? What is the best month for popcorn sales? What is the best month for potato chips? Use the information plotted on this line graph to answer the questions below.

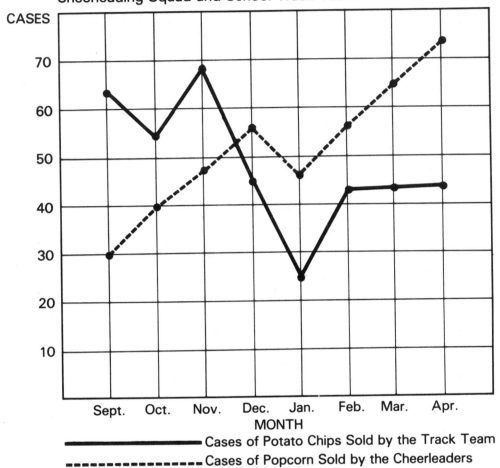

POPCORN & POTATO CHIP SALES:
Cheerleading Squad and School Track Team

▬▬▬ Cases of Potato Chips Sold by the Track Team
▬ ▬ ▬ Cases of Popcorn Sold by the Cheerleaders

1. Which group had the highest sales in the month of September? _____

2. Which group had the highest sales in the month of January? _____

3. How many cases of popcorn did the cheerleaders sell in March? _____

4. How many cases of potato chips did the track team sell in November? _____

5. Which group had the lowest-selling month? _____

6. The sales program came to an end in April. Which group was making the most sales by the end of the selling program? _____

ACTIVITY 16
Reading a bar graph

Another type of graph is the bar graph. Here is an example of a bar graph.

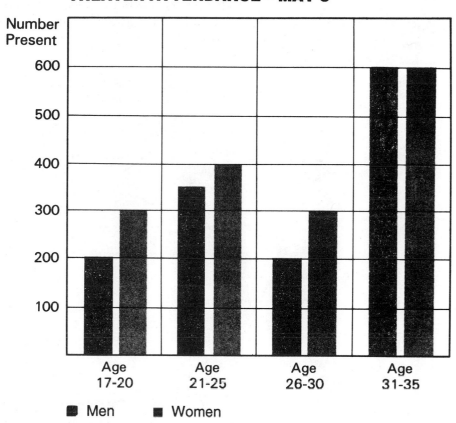

THEATER ATTENDANCE – MAY 5

Number Present

- ■ Men
- ■ Women

Use the graph to answer these questions.

1. How many women between 17 and 20 attended the theater on May 5? _____

2. How many men between 17 and 20? _____

3. Which age group had the highest attendance on May 5? _____

4. What was the total attendance for the 26–30 age group? _____

5. Which age group, including men and women, had more than 500 present? _____

6. Which age groups had the same overall attendance on May 5? _____

7. What was the total attendance for the 17–20 age group on May 5? _____

8. On May 5, did more men or more women attend the theater? _____

ACTIVITY 17
Reading a circle graph

A circle graph shows the relationship of parts to a whole. You can divide a circle into sections. Then you can compare one section with another. You can also compare one section with the whole circle. Look at the budget circle below.

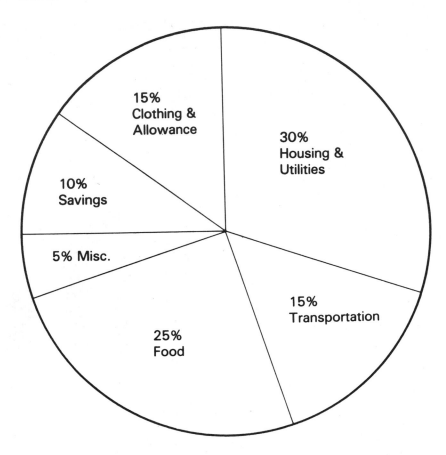

This graph shows how the Jacksons, a family of three, spend their yearly income. The questions that follow are about the Jacksons' budget circle. Choose the letter that correctly answers each question.

_____ 1. How much of the Jacksons' budget goes toward housing and utilities?
    a. 10%   **c.** 30%
    b. 20%   **d.** 40%

_____ 2. What percent do they save?
    a. 10%   **c.** 30%
    b. 20%   **d.** 5%

_____ 3. Which two sections make up a little more than half of the Jacksons' budget?
    a. Savings and Food
    b. Food and Transportation
    c. Miscellaneous (Misc.) and Food
    d. Housing & Utilities and Food

_____ 4. Which section is the smallest part of the budget?
    a. Transportation
    b. Miscellaneous (Misc.)
    c. Food
    d. Clothing & Allowances

_____ 5. If the Jacksons' budget got too tight, which of these items could they eliminate?
    a. Housing & Utilities
    b. Food
    c. Transportation
    d. Savings

Study the circle and bar graphs below.

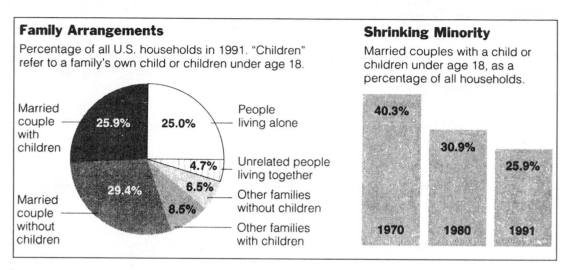

Family Arrangements

Percentage of all U.S. households in 1991. "Children" refer to a family's own child or children under age 18.

- Married couple with children — 25.9%
- People living alone — 25.0%
- Unrelated people living together — 4.7%
- Other families without children — 6.5%
- Other families with children — 8.5%
- Married couple without children — 29.4%

Shrinking Minority

Married couples with a child or children under age 18, as a percentage of all households.

- 1970 — 40.3%
- 1980 — 30.9%
- 1991 — 25.9%

Source: U.S. Census Bureau

1. Look at the circle graph. What percentage of people in the United States live alone? _____

2. Which percentage is greater—married couples with children or married couples without children?

   _____

3. Add the percentage of married couples with children to the percentage of married couples without children. Is the total number of married couples over or under 50 percent? _____

4. Look at the bar graph. What was the percentage of married couples with a child or children in 1970?

   _____

5. Was the decrease shown on the bar graph greater between 1970 and 1980 or between 1980 and 1991? _____

SHOW WHAT YOU KNOW . . .

About Charts and Graphs

Turn back to the temperature chart on page 51. On a sheet of graph paper make a bar graph showing the average maximum and minimum temperatures for Cape Hatteras. Use the graph on page 55 as a model. Label your graph and show a key.

HINT: Show the temperatures on a vertical axis in multiples of 5, beginning with 35° at the bottom. Show months on the horizontal axis.

ANSWER KEY

Using Directories

ACTIVITY 1—Using Store Directories (p. 2)
1. 3 2. 1 3. 2 4. 2 5. 2 6. 2 7. 1 8. 1 9. 2 10. 3 11. 2
12. 3 13. 2 14. 2 15. 1 16. 1 17. 1 18. 2 19. 3 20. 3
21. 1 22. 3 23. 2 24. 1 25. 1 or (3) 26. 2 27. 1 28. 1 29. 2
30. 1

ACTIVITY 2—Using a Floor Directory for a Department Store (p. 3)
1. seventh
2. fifth
3. second if you are female; third if you are male
4. third
5. fourth
6. fifth
7. sixth
8. fourth
9. seventh
10. seventh

ACTIVITY 3—Using Building Directories (p. 4)
1. 10; 10
2. 10
3. no
4. yes
5. 10
6. yes
7. Martin Wholesalers
8. Marvel Photos
9. one
10. one
11. 6
12. a. 708
    b. 502
    c. 611
    d. 613
    e. 707
    f. 605
    g. 1013
    h. 510

ACTIVITY 4—Using Floor Plans (p. 6)
1. West
2. two
3. yes
4. yes
5. east and north
6. ten
7. no
8. yes

Check Your Understanding of Directories and Floor Plans (p. 7)
1. alphabetically
2. left
3. right
4. mezzanine
5. Daisy's Donut Shop, A–1
6. Norge's Portraits, B–2

ACTIVITY 5—Reading the White Pages (p. 9)
1. 555-8332
2. 555-4149
3. 555-8866
4. 555-3321
5. 555-7899
6. 555-8254

ACTIVITY 6—Locating Telephone Numbers for Persons with the Same Names (p. 9)
1. 555-2813
2. 555-3245
3. 555-6471
4. three
5. 555-7110
6. 555-3331

ACTIVITY 7—Deciding When to Use the Yellow Pages (p. 10)
1. Answers will vary but may include: easy to locate all businesses offering the service, product, or specialty you are looking for; easy to find store that is most conveniently located; may be able to find out hours; may be able to get directions; may be able to call ahead and check if item is available.
2. yellow pages
3. white pages (Since you already know the name of the shop, the white pages should be faster.)

ACTIVITY 8—Classifying Yellow-Page Listings (p. 11)
Furniture Listings
1. c 2. c 3. a 4. b 5. b 6. a (sometimes b) 7. a 8. b 9. c
10. a
Car Businesses
1. d 2. d 3. b 4. b 5. d 6. d 7. a 8. d 9. d 10. a
11. c 12. e 13. c 14. a 15. e 16. c

ACTIVITY 9—Reading and Understanding the Yellow Pages (p. 12)
1. dry cleaners
2. DeLuxe Dry Cleaners Plant
3. Sudden Service Cleaners
4. yes (heading says *Cleaners—Cont'd.*)
5. a service
6. Phyl's One Hour Martinizing
7. Mr. Suds Dry Cleaning; Querbach Leather Process Inc.; Suburban Dry Cleaners & Shirt Launderers
8. Guida Dry Cleaners
9. Realgood Cleaners

ACTIVITY 10— Choosing the Yellow Pages or the White Pages (p. 13)
1. a 2. c 3. c 4. a 5. c 6. a 7. c 8. b 9. a 10. b
11. c 12. c 13. a 14. c 15. a 16. b 17. c 18. c 19. c
20. c

ACTIVITY 11—Reading Area Code Maps (p. 13)
1. Arizona, 602; South Dakota, 605; Wyoming, 307; Utah, 801
2. Alaska, 907; Hawaii, 808; Bermuda, 809; Puerto Rico, 809
3. Ontario Canada, 807, 705, 519, 416, 613; Quebec, 819, 418, 514; Saskatchewan, 306
4. Florida—four (904, 407, 305, 813); West Virginia—one (304); Georgia—three (404, 706, 912); Montana—one (406); Texas—eight (806, 817, 915, 214, 903, 713, 409, 512)
5. San Antonio (512); Houston (713); Dallas (214)
6. 215
7. 404

ACTIVITY 12—Reading Area Code Maps (p. 15)
Situation #1
A. Mr. Brown just left for lunch. New York time: 12:01 P.M.
Situation #2
C. Call back in an hour. Des Moines time: 2:00 P.M.

Check Your Understanding of Telephone Directories (p. 16)
1. S
2. Carpenters
3. Bus lines
4. look under Plumbing; Plumbers; or Plumbing & Heating.
5. P (or Pierce)
6. 10:30 A.M.
7. b
8. MacDonald; Mack; Major; McKay; McNeil; Miner
9. Avenue
10. one home number and one office number

Special Reading Strategies

ACTIVITY 1—Identifying Regulatory Signs (p. 20)
1. C 2. A 3. E 4. H 5. B 6. F 7. D 8. G 9. I

ACTIVITY 2—Identifying Warning Signs (p. 23)
1. G 2. D 3. H 4. F 5. B 6. I 7. C 8. A 9. K 10. E

ACTIVITY 3—Identifying Street and Highway Signs (p. 25)
1st row: regulatory, regulatory, service and guide
2nd row: warning, warning, service and guide

Check Your Understanding of Street and Highway Signs (p. 26)
1. No U turn
2. Curve ahead
3. Intersection—watch for cars crossing, entering, or leaving highway
4. Picnic table
5. No right turn
6. Watch for schoolchildren
7. No trucks
8. A bridge or underpass ahead; clearance is 12 feet, 6 inches
9. Hill—drivers must take special care
10. Traffic may be moving into your lane; be ready to change your speed or lane.

SHOW WHAT YOU KNOW... About Street and Highway Signs (p. 27)
Groups' signs will vary.

ACTIVITY 4—Understanding a Trail Map (p. 30)
1. 5 miles
2. Difficult and Moderate
3. Moderate
4. yes
5. one
6. west
7. back
8. left

ACTIVITY 5—Understanding a Map Legend (p. 31)
1. state highway
2. railroad
3. interstate route
4. state park
5. freeway or tollway (Note: On a four-color map, the symbol for freeway is in one color and the symbol for tollway is in another.)
6. U.S. route number
7. airport
8. county seat
9. state trail
10. state tourist information center

SHOW WHAT YOU KNOW... About Street and Highway Signs (p. 32)
Answers will vary.

ACTIVITY 6—Understanding a Street Map (p. 33)
1. Woodward
2. Municipal Courts
3. Wayne County Community College
4. yes
5. interstate highway
6. six; five
7. east/west
8. no

ACTIVITY 7—Finding Locations with an Index and Grid (p. 36)
1. south
2. Olive
3. two
4. B–3
5. one
6. southeast
7. left
8. left
9. Take Lime north to Alhambra and turn west, or take San Miguel west to Plum and go north to Alhambra and turn east.
10. El Camino, Canyon, and Rodeo

ACTIVITY 8—Understanding a State Highway Map (p. 37)
1. 94
2. 18
3. Big Foot Beach and Bong Recreation Area
4. Kettle Moraine State Forest
5. yes
6. yes
7. yes
8. Orfordville; Magnolia
9. smaller
10. yes

Check Your Understanding of Maps (p. 38)
1. 83
2. 95
3. 895 (Harob Tunnel) or 695 (Francis Scott Key Bridge)
4. southeast
5. 695
6. Patapsco Valley State Park
7. Take Route 1 north to Route 40 east into Baltimore.
8. Major routes only are shown.

SHOW WHAT YOU KNOW... About Mapping a Route (p. 39)
Answers will vary.

ACTIVITY 9—Understanding Timetables (p. 42)
1. eight
2. 372 miles or 599 kilometers
3. 63
4. The Niagara Rainbow
5. 8:40 A.M.
6. 11:30 P.M.
7. Albany-Rensselaer
8. 11:27 A.M.
9. 4:40 P.M.
10. evening

ACTIVITY 10—Understanding Timetables (p. 43)
1. Augusta: 88/918; 4:25 P.M.; 6:25 P.M.; 1.
Charleston: 60; 8:10 A.M.; 8:52 A.M.; 0.
Columbia: 88/918; 4:25 P.M.; 7:01 P.M.; 2.
2. Atlanta: 5; Chicago: 3; Columbus: 1.
3. #943
4. Atlanta
5. #951
6. Atlanta; Charleston; Charlotte; Fayetteville/Fort Bragg; Greenville/Spartanburg; Hickory/Lenoir/Morganton; Knoxville/Oak Ridge (any four)
7. Saturdays
8. #24/927

ACTIVITY 11—Reading an Airport Terminal Schedule (p. 45)
1. 3:10; yes
2. 3:00; no
3. Flight #49; Flight #74; Flight #39
4. no; the plane is landing
5. 4:15; no
6. no
7. yes; 33
8. #412
9. Detroit

ACTIVITY 12—Understanding Timetables (p. 46)
1. Philadelphia and Ocean City
2. down
3. up
4. 10:05
5. 6:05; 6:35
6. 6:50; 8:25; 8:40
7. State Road, DE
8. 1st stop: Salisbury; 2nd stop: Milford; 3rd stop: Harrington; 4th stop: Dover; 5th stop: Smyrna
9. 3:35
10. 7:05

Check Your Understanding of Timetables (p. 48)
Down:
1. The Pioneer
2. 25; 26
3. 11:25 P
4. 12:20 A
5. 12:35 A
6. 11:10 A; 1:30 P; 6:00 P; 6:21 P
7. 9:50 P

Up:
1. 7:10 A
2. Tacoma
3. 11:00 A
4. 11:10 A
5. Ontario
6. 7:10 A

SHOW WHAT YOU KNOW... About Timetables (p. 49)
The train takes 22 hours to go 1081 miles. Average speed is 49 mph.

ACTIVITY 13—Reading a Temperature Chart (p. 51)
1. 54
2. 36
3. 93
4. December
5. August
6. Florence, SC
7. Asheville, NC
8. Savannah, GA

ACTIVITY 14—Reading a Recreation Site Chart (p. 52)
1. across
2. down
3. no
4. Beach Fork, Bluestone, Hawks Nest, Pricketts Fort, Tygart Lake
5. Blackwater Falls, Cacapon, Tygart Lake
6. the letter *N*

ACTIVITY 15—Reading a Line Graph (p. 54)
1. the track team
2. the cheerleaders
3. 65
4. 68
5. the track team
6. the cheerleaders

ACTIVITY 16—Reading a Bar Graph (p. 55)
1. 300
2. 200
3. 31–35
4. 500
5. 31–35
6. 17–20 and 26–30 age groups
7. 500
8. women

ACTIVITY 17—Reading a Circle Graph (p. 56)
1. c 2. a 3. d 4. b 5. d

Check Your Understanding of Graphs (p. 57)
1. 25%
2. married couple without children
3. over 50%
4. 40.3%
5. between 1970 and 1980

SHOW WHAT YOU KNOW... About Charts and Graphs (p. 58)
Answers should show understanding of a bar graph.

A Visit to
Washington, D.C.

By Jill Krementz

SCHOLASTIC INC.
New York Toronto London Auckland Sydney

Also by Jill Krementz

The Face of South Vietnam
(with text by Dean Brelis)

Sweet Pea—A Black Girl
Growing Up in the Rural South

Words and Their Masters
(with text by Israel Shenker)

A Very Young Dancer

A Very Young Rider

A Very Young Gymnast

A Very Young Circus Flyer

A Very Young Skater

The Writer's Image

How It Feels When a Parent Dies

How It Feels To Be Adopted

How It Feels When Parents Divorce

The Fun of Cooking

Lily Goes to the Playground

Jack Goes to the Beach

Taryn Goes to the Dentist

Benjy Goes to a Restaurant

Katherine Goes to Nursery School

Jamie Goes on an Airplane

Zachary Goes to the Zoo

Holly's Farm Animals

Photograph of Ling-Ling and Hsing-Hsing by Jessie Cohen.
Reprinted courtesy of the Office of Graphics and Exhibits,
National Zoological Park

ISBN 0-590-40583-7

This book is dedicated to Chris Downey, with much love.

Acknowledgments

My thanks to the following people for their help:

Mike Fuller, my resourceful and always dependable lighting assistant; and Bill Geiger, who also assisted.

My office assistant, Robert Hajek, who kept everything organized.

Laura Perry, the sort of editorial assistant every writer dreams about.

Leigh Anne Donahue, Staff Assistant to Senator Joseph R. Biden.

Congressman Tom Downey, his wife Chris Downey, and their daughter Lauren.

Joanne Puglisi, appointments secretary and office manager for Congressman Downey.

John Brademas, George Nicholson, Ole Risom, Tom Jackson, Fred Gerard, Peggy Cafritz, and Kurt Vonnegut, who looked at this book before it went to press and offered valuable suggestions.

Jack Russ, Sergeant at Arms in the House of Representatives; and Sergeant Warren Hurlock, who was especially helpful.

J. Carter Brown, Director at the National Gallery of Art; and Ellen Stanley, Programs Assistant in the Information Office.

At the Washington Cathedral: Nancy S. Montgomery, Communications Director; Linda Freeman; Ann Etches, Manager of the Cathedral's Brass Rubbing Workshop.

Sergeant First Class Woodrow English, Bugler at The Tomb of the Unknown Soldier.

Janet Pawlukiewicz, Office of Education at the National Museum of Natural History. She is the Manager of the Discovery Room.

Margie Gibson, Office of Public Affairs at the National Zoological Park.

Joyce Dall'Acqua, Office of Public Affairs and Museum Services at the National Air and Space Museum; and Tracy Jackson, Office of Protection Services.

Florian H. Thayn, Head, Art and Reference Division, at the Office of the Architect of the Capitol.

At the Bureau of Engraving and Printing: Robert Leuver, Director; Linda Coleman and Leah Akbar, Public Affairs Staff; Donald A. D'Agostino, Office of Security; Delores V. Briscoe and Emma M. Forbes, Currency Examiners.

Alberto Ocampo, Manager of Axxion Copy, who spent many hours with me making color xeroxes from my transparencies while I worked on the layouts for this book.

The always gracious staff at The Four Seasons Hotel.

At Scholastic: Jean Feiwel, Frances Leos, Rose-Ellen Lorber-Termaat, Nancy Pines, Emmeline Hsi, and Diana Hrisinko.

Most of all, I am indebted to the Wilson Family—Matt, Cole, Martha, and Bob. They were a joy to work with and they are a pleasure to know.

My name's Matt Wilson, and I'm six years old. I live in Washington, D.C. That's the Capitol building behind me. It's where the members of Congress make the laws. Most of the U.S. government is in Washington. The city was named for General George Washington, who was the first President of our country.

One of the best things about living in Washington is that
I've learned so much about the history of our country.

My whole family enjoys sightseeing—Daddy, Mommy,
and my little brother Cole.

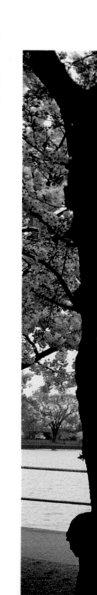

There are lots of monuments to Presidents, like the one to Thomas Jefferson. It's fun to look at it from up in the cherry trees. They're very good for climbing.

In the spring, people come to Washington to see the trees' pink blossoms, which only last a few weeks. They were given to America by the Japanese.

One statue perfect for climbing is the one of Albert Einstein.
He was a famous scientist who changed the way we think
about the universe.

Sometimes I whisper a secret in his ear.

On the west front of the Capitol building is another great climbing statue of soldiers fighting in the Civil War. It's called the Grant Memorial.

I like to sit on a horse and yell, "Charge!"

Some monuments honor soldiers
who fought and died for America.
At the Vietnam Memorial there is
a list on shining black granite of
all the men and women who were
lost in that war.

Daddy's older brother died in Vietnam,
so this is a very special place for our
family to visit.

My dad always likes to touch my
uncle's name with his fingers.

Sometimes people leave flowers at the
foot of the wall.

There's a statue at the Vietnam Memorial, too. It's of three soldiers like my uncle, and they look very real.

If you go behind them you can see their canteens
and the bullets they had to carry.

My dad says sometimes we don't know the names of all the soldiers who died. At Arlington Cemetery there is a memorial for them, too. It's called the Tomb of the Unknown Soldier.

They have a changing of the guard every half hour. When this happens, all the visitors are told to "stand and remain silent."

The soldiers are very good at shining their shoes, polishing their brass, and cleaning their guns. Their blue uniforms are called "blues."

Their shoes have "cheaters" on them, which make a really loud noise when they click their heels together.

When the bugler plays taps everybody stands up very straight.
It makes me feel proud of my country.

One time I got to shake hands with him.

One of the nicest places in Washington is the Botanic Gardens.
It's like being in an indoor jungle.

My favorite flowers
are the orchids. They
smell wonderful.

There are all kinds of
exotic plants with names
like "Painted Lady."

NEOREGELIA HYBRID CV.
PAINTED LADY
BROMELIACEAE

I never knew there were so many sizes and shapes of cactus plants.
But they all have one thing in common: They're prickly!

One cactus is so tall they cut a hole in the roof to let it out.

Sometimes we feed the ducks at the Reflecting Pool. It reflects the Washington Monument, named after George Washington.

The monument has flags all the way around it. You can ride to the top in an elevator and sometimes they let you walk down the 898 steps.

Cole and I play in the fields nearby. In the spring when the daffodils are in bloom, we have to be careful not to step on them.

The mall's a big lawn in the middle of all the monuments, and the merry-go-round there is definitely worth a visit.

Near the merry-go-round, in the National Museum of Natural History,
is one of our favorite places—the Discovery Room. It's called that
because you can explore and discover lots of things there.

One wall has boxes full of things like Indian dolls, animal skulls,
bark from trees, coral from the ocean, spices, sea urchin shells, and frogs.

It's such a relaxing place that lots of the grown-ups call it the "Recovery Room."

You can look at and touch everything, including a microscope anyone can use. Cole's fingernail looked really weird!

In one corner they have a collection of costumes you can try on. They're from many different countries. The Indian gloves have cuffs that are decorated with tiny beads. The moccasins smell like smoke because they're made from smoked moose hide.

It's a great place to meet other kids. Or a crocodile!

We explore at the Air and Space Museum, too. I love this place because it's full of airplanes, rockets, missiles, and space capsules. They even have the suits that our astronauts wore when they were in space.

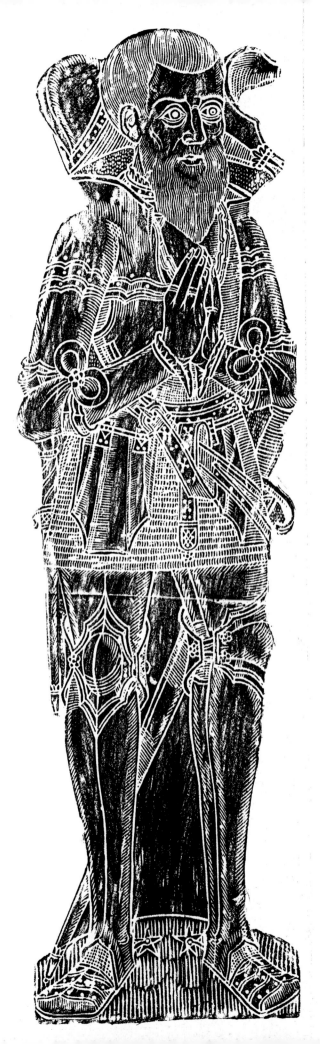

I also like the suits of armor that knights wore in medieval times.

In the workshop at the Washington Cathedral you can make a brass rubbing of a knight in armor with crayons made from beeswax.

I made a rubbing of Edward, the Black Prince.

If you like money, be sure to visit the Bureau of Engraving and Printing! Dollar bills—ones, fives, tens, twenties, fifties, and hundreds—all come off the printing presses in big sheets. Then they're checked for mistakes before they are cut into single bills.

I learned a lot about our currency. All bills say "In God We Trust" on them and they aren't made out of paper. They're made of 75 percent cotton and 25 percent linen, which is why they last so long. Paper money would only last a week!

The Bureau of Engraving and Printing makes about 6.2 billion dollar bills a year. The ink on them never completely dries. If you rub a bill on a piece of white paper with your thumbnail, the ink will come off.

Andrew Jackson is on the twenty dollar bill. Do you know which bill George Washington is on?

The National Gallery of Art has another picture of George Washington.
Mom said he's not smiling because he had wooden teeth, which didn't fit
very well. She asked me if I'd like to wear a powdered wig with a little bow.

I said, "No way!"

The reason there are so many presidential monuments and statues in Washington is because most of the Presidents lived in this city.

The White House was built in 1792. John Adams, our second President, moved there in 1800, and that's where all the Presidents have lived ever since. You can take guided tours through the White House during special hours.

Thomas Jefferson was our third President, and he was also a famous architect. His monument looks like the kind of houses he used to build.

The huge statue of Jefferson inside the monument is Cole's favorite.

At the Lincoln Memorial there's a gigantic statue of Abraham Lincoln sitting in a chair. I learned about him at school. He was the 16th President and he stopped slavery.

President John F. Kennedy's grave has a flame that never goes out so we'll always remember him. It's called the Eternal Flame. I asked my dad what keeps the fire burning all the time. He said it's oil. At night the flame is especially pretty.

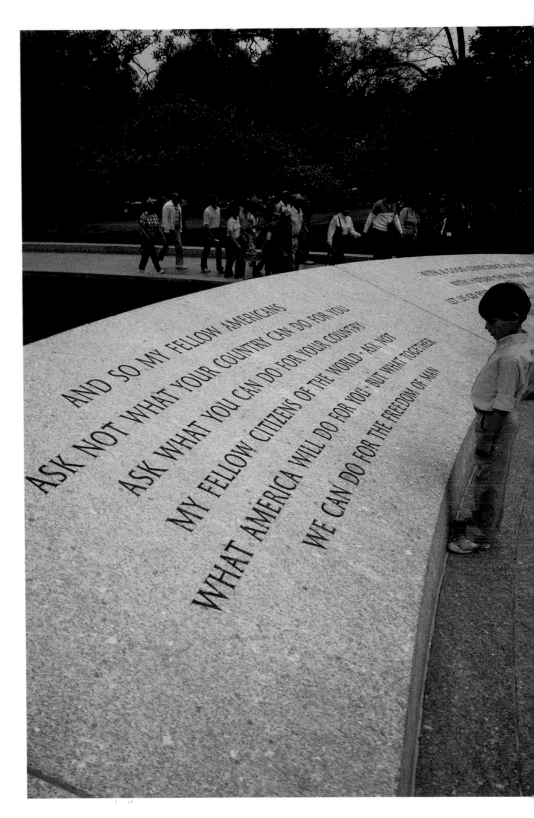

President Kennedy's most famous sayings
are set in stone nearby.

The Eternal Flame is at Arlington Cemetery. Lots of generals and other important people are buried there. It's actually in Virginia on a beautiful hill that overlooks the Potomac River and Washington on the other side.

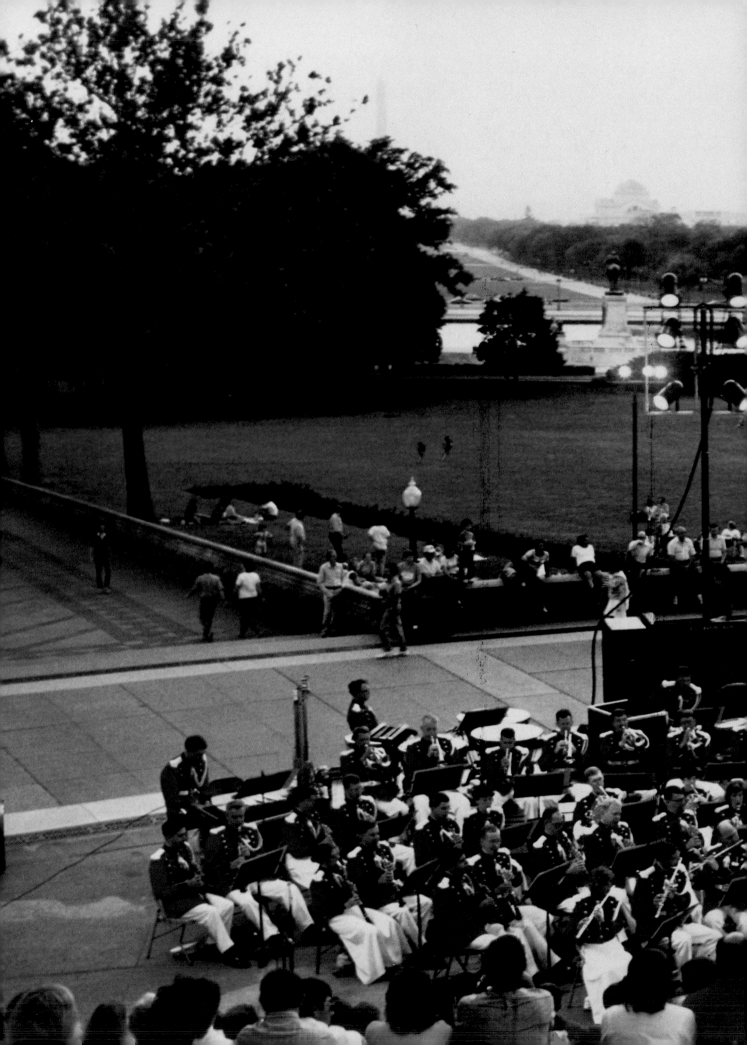

If you come to Washington during the summer, be sure to end the day with a visit to the Capitol grounds where you can listen to a military band and watch the sun set. Sometimes we bring a picnic supper.

There are so many exciting things to see and do in Washington, D.C.
If I tried to tell you about all of them, this book would be a million pages long.
I've told you about some of our favorite places!

There are maps everywhere, which make it easy to find other museums
and monuments. Or you might want to visit the pandas from China at the
National Zoo or see the old railway cars at the Museum of American History.

Don't forget your camera. I know you'll have a great time!

Capitol Building
Capitol Hill
(202) 225-6827
Guided tours daily,
9:00 A.M.-3:45 P.M.
Closed Thanksgiving, Christmas Day, and
New Year's Day

Jefferson Memorial
South Bank, Tidal Basin
(202) 426-6841
Daily, 8:00 A.M.-Midnight
Japanese Cherry Trees
Tidal Basin

Albert Einstein Statue
Outside of National Academy of Sciences
22nd Street and Constitution Avenue, NW

The Grant Memorial
West Front, Capitol Building

Vietnam Memorial
Mall, near 23rd Street, NW
(202) 426-6841
Daily, 8:00 A.M.-Midnight

Tomb of the Unknown Soldier
Arlington Cemetery
Arlington, VA
(202) 692-0931
Daily, 8:00 A.M.-5:00 P.M.
Changing of the guard every hour; every
half hour during the summer.

Botanic Gardens
Maryland Avenue, between 1st and 2nd
Streets, SW
(202) 225-7099
Open daily, 9:00 A.M.-5:00 P.M.

Washington Monument, Reflecting Pool
Mall at 15th Street, NW
(202) 426-6841
Daily, March 20-Labor Day, 8:00 A.M.-Midnight
Day after Labor Day-March 19, 9:00 A.M.-
5:00 P.M.

Carousel
Mall, across from Arts & Industries Building
A Smithsonian Museum
900 Jefferson Drive, SW
(703) 560-2846
May-Aug., M-F, 10:00 A.M.-4:30 P.M.
Sat & Sun, 10:00 A.M.-5:30 P.M.
Sept., open weekends only
Closed Oct.-May 1st

Discovery Room
National Museum of Natural History
A Smithsonian Museum
10th Street and Constitution Avenue, NW
(202) 357-2695
M-Th, 12:00 P.M.-2:30 P.M.
F-Sun, 10:30 A.M.-3:30 P.M.

The National Air and Space Museum
A Smithsonian Museum
7th Street and Independence Avenue, SW
(202) 357-2020, 357-2700
Open daily, 10:00 A.M.-5:30 P.M.
Closed Christmas Day